For all who wants to become children...

The Treasure of the Heavens

by Dr. Rafael González

DEDICATION

To my Lord and Savior Jesus Christ for giving me life with His Mercy after all the doctors twice told my wife and my mother to prepare for a funeral, to my wife Maria for surrendering all of her tears to Jesus in my death bed and surrendering herself to the Merciful Will of God, to my mother Amaury who damaged both of her knees praying, pleading each moment for a recovery miracle, for my Kids Rafael, Ignahi and Axel who gives me joy for being alive, for my sisters Ignahi, Virginia, Lisa, Dianne, Rita, my brothers Gustavo, Ruben Gomez and Franklin; for all who prayed for a Miracle to Jesus and getting one after I woke up from an induced coma... to Mary the Mother of Jesus for the sweetest hug ever while praying the rosary returning for good to the USA, to The Holy Spirit for giving me the Mercy of Jesus into my unworthy heart every day, to all of my brothers in Christ specially Mariano and Clara Rivera who prayed for me when I needed the most, to my evangelical brothers who love Christ... Julie and family, Kathy and Manuel, Henry Campusano and Family; to my brothers in our Catholic faith specially all the old members from "El grupo la paz de Cristo" in Santo Domingo, Dominican Republic to Smeling and Flavio Grullón and their respective families; to father Wilson Salazar in Colombia and his teachings, father Angel from the order of the Passionists in Puerto Rico for being a friend, father Edward Wal of the Transfiguration church and his patience with me, to Monsignor Harry Bumpus may God bless his soul, to Michael Voris for keeping me fed in the faith, also for the Spirit FM crew for giving me joy through the Rosary, The whole Stetson University family, Chief Howard, Viegname Somado and his family, Tafari Brown my brother, Camilo Rodriguez and family and Charles Deonarinesingh and to all who love Christ... I dedicate this work to you all.

The Treasure of the Heavens: The biggest robbery in history and the art of war books was reviewed by Reverend Monsignor Harold Bumpus (1931-2013) God bless his soul, he said about the book: "This is a good spiritual book because it reflects the teachings of the bible." Please say a Hail Mary for Msgr. Harry Bumpus also If you like this book GET ONE FOR ANYBODY WHO HAS FALLEN AWAY FROM THE FAITH, or anybody you hold dear and needs encouragement in the faith; you can contact me for anything, from prayer that you might need or testimonies you would like to share at doctorgonzalez@live.com   May Jesus gives you and your family tons of His Sweet Mercy. Amen

BOOK I:

THE BIGGEST ROBBERY IN HISTORY.

PREFACE

Being a thief is like an art said Dismas: "you have to take things without them knowing you were ever there". Dismas was the leader of two that took whatever they wanted from the people of Egypt without getting much attention; he embraced the life of a thief, not because he wanted to but because that's all he knew as he grew up without a father. The romans took his father away by the force of the sword, he didn't like to make his Mother Helen suffer because of his criminal ways, but Helen suffered indeed because she didn't see her son as a criminal, she saw him as her sweet boy... Egypt was tough, Dismas and Mother Helen ran from the claws of King Herod, they came to Egypt looking for refuge as they thought that all Jews were being annihilated. It wasn't easy times for the Jews everywhere, Jews felt oppressed every day and they always tried to rise against the aggressor... Dismas were making things difficult for his Mother whom he loved greatly, so he prepared to leave his wicked ways for the love he had for Helen. Helen lost the perfect husband to the barbaric ways of the Romans, so she always had to remind her son about his father, Simon; Dismas was always remembered by Helen where he came from, how his father was and how Helen unconsciously wants her son to become: a good man. They decided to go back home, but it wasn't Bethlehem, Dismas insisted to go to the big city: The Holy city of Jerusalem. Dismas was a an adult already even though his Mother saw him as a child, they went to Jerusalem as Dismas promised to leave his criminal ways behind, but they didn't know that Dismas was ready to pulled his biggest job ever! Stealing the biggest treasure of them all, the treasure of the heavens right there in Jerusalem.

PROLOGUE

It is all good my Lord, as I watch the stars shining more than ever, my Helen and my son were in my Heart illuminating me as they sleep, I thank You I AM for the beauty of life which comes only from your hands, I thank You for my family my sweet Lord and King of the celestial armies your Mercy is not only legendary but real, I beg You to let me defend my family not with swords, spears or rocks, but only with Your Wisdom... I praise You tonight and always I AM because you have given me more than riches, you have given me Your Love through my Helen and my son; I Simon, son of Aaron and Rebecca, sheepherder and farmer, a nobody between kings, wiseman and ordinary man, I need to declare onto You my great God that me and my house are Yours forever, I know that is not much but I want to thank You properly I AM, my soul and my family are Yours even if we are only us three, You know that I can't speak for my brother Benjamin who despises me, even though... bless him my Lord with Your Mercy, I beg You. What a beautiful night my Lord, it's been days since that beautiful star shined like the sun in the middle of the night here in Bethlehem, my God I AM... please never forget Your servant and his family, I always preserved Your commandments because I Love You Lord, please don't hide from us, don't move away from us and show us the beauty of Your Mercy, this I beg You for the Glory and Honor of Your Name. Amen.

Cough! Cough...Cough!, Oh God it's so hard to breathe right now! The crowd is here and they're pleased to see a good show, some people watching and enjoying the misfortunes of some... in this case me!... Others... very few, with tears in their eyes and some in disbelief... Cough! Cough! Oh my sweet God these nails hurt so much...How did I got here? How did I got into this mess? Thank God that my parents are dead so they wouldn't see this gathering... Yes I got caught alright that's what happened and this is what I got for my transgressions, I look up into the sun and I remember when everything was... well, how I came to be. Memories of the past come hard with this pain eating me up inside but when it comes to mind, it's wonderful... I see my Mother telling me how father use to be... he was a good man, I don't remember much of him because I was only two years old when I lost him, my Mother never allowed me to forget him, always telling me how he was and the story of how I got saved from King Herod. I was little then, he used to work in somebody's land farming and watching some sheep, while my mother took care of me in our house. We were living in Bethlehem, Mother used to tell me this story like thousand times, so I wouldn't forget... she said that my father one afternoon came back running home dressed in red, funny thing said my Mother he went out in his white farming piece and he came in mostly red, my Mother crying and shouting said...

- "What happened? Is this your blood?"

- "No, it's not mine (He replied), we need to go now...we need to go now..., do not ask questions just trust what I say... take the boy, let's go!"

My father quickly washed the blood of his face, hands, and change some of his clothes, then he took us out through the back, we got to the very edge of our town, we waited behind some house as night came creeping in, my mother was worried because of all the shouting and crying in the distance ... people crying like they were being tortured!

- "What is going on Simon?... What is happening?"

- Simon: "Quiet woman... There's danger everywhere we need to be silent."

- Simon: (whispering) "As you know I was watching some sheep, when I got back I saw the Romans from a distance they were at the house of the Levi family that live near the well, all of our friends were dead in the ground!... the Romans didn't see me, one of them shout:

- "We are taking the town by night fall so all resistance could be easy to eliminate!"

- Simon: "I guess that they grew tired of all Israel, so I'm not taking chances we're headed to Egypt."

Mother told me this story thousands of times, she always had to fight the tears, it broke my heart every time even though I knew the whole story, I just let her tell it like it was the first time, for my Mother was very important so I never refused, never! I know that she didn't want me to forget my Father and what he did for us.

As we got nearer to the outside of the town, the crying, the shouting, the screaming seemed irrelevant to my father, he was determined to free his family from the horror of the Romans, suddenly, we saw three soldiers were coming our way, fortunately they haven't spotted us yet! My father said to my Mother.

- Simon: "I will try to make them follow me, so you could get through to the fields, avoid all roads, run through the hills and don't stop till you get somewhere safe, if you can get to Egypt safe, it'll be the best... I'll meet you there my love, please be strong... please, This is the only way..."

My Mother resisted the idea, because the Romans were beasts… famous for their lack of Mercy and if they get their hands on my father, it'll be his end.

- Mother: "How can you let little Dismas and me go alone, if you die, I'll die too… please don't go Simon…"

- Simon: "My sweet Helen you have given me a Sea of love, but now is not the time for this…it's the time to think about the future of our little Son… I love you Helen, I love you little Dismas…"

- Simon: "Now go, as soon as they pass you by… run as far away as you can, God willing we'll be together… go to your aunt's house in Egypt I'll meet you there, run and don't stop…"

My father then kissed my Mother and me, he went out the road and shouted to the Romans "Beasts", he started to run away while the three Romans chased him, my Mother and I ran out of town towards freedom and uncertainty. We ran through the night and it wasn't an easy task Mother says, a woman and her two year old son running through the fields fearing the worst… it was the longest night of our lives according to my Mother… we were running from the Romans on foot for long and then walked even more until the next morning, there was no break for us because we didn't want to get killed, we walked and walked until finally… we got lucky; a caravan going exactly where we were going, Egypt.

- Helen: "Praise I AM for His Mercy, because we didn't fall into the hands of the Romans and I'm sure that His Mercy will take care of your father and return him to you my little Dismas, blessed is His Name".

The killing of the children in Bethlehem that's what we knew then it happened in our town, the word got out in a hurry that king Herod executed young children with less than 2 years of age, some people weren't surprised at all as the King killed one of his sons, many of Jews got killed because they didn't want to let their sons be executed, in the confusion some Romans even killed children above that age threshold even little girls...Beasts!.

We got to Egypt, but something strange was happening with my Mother, she was worried... worried about my father and even more worried because of me, she found out that same day I had some sort of a rash in one of my arms that kept on growing, it spread to my chest and she feared the worst, she knew that if the people within the caravan find out that I have a skin disease, they could leave us behind or even kill us. We were already past the Egypt border, we were staying put for the night, since my mother couldn't stop sobbing, and a lady from the tent in front of us came to her.

- Lady: "Peace be with you... why are you so sad?, is there anything that I could do for you?, is the boy all right?...

-Helen: "I'm sorry, I'm sorry I have put you in danger... my son is sick and I fear that it's something very, very bad in his skin, I'm sorry"

The Lady smiled and said to my Mother...

- Lady: "Please don't be afraid... for God there's no impossible... please trust me and come, please come."

- Helen: "But that skin disease is very infectious."

- Lady: "Please trust I AM and come."

- Helen: "....."

Once inside the little improvised tent they had, she saw a man sleeping with a baby in his arms.

- Lady: "I just bathe my son a little while ago, please go ahead and use the same water that I use to bathe him... I'm sure that you love God and He will not forsake you in this foreign land... trust me and bathe your son now with these water and I know that everything will be alright, I pray for you to see God's Sweet Mercy".

-Helen: "I don't understand..."

- Lady: "Don't be afraid; lay your trust into the Lord's hands."

- Helen: "I thank you, God knows that it's a fact that my Dismas need some cleaning, it's been a while you know ha, ha, ha..."

- Helen: (As she started to clean little Dismas with the waters). "Please I must know your name."

- Lady: "My name is Mary and this is my family, the sleepy head there is my husband Joseph and the baby in his arms is our son Jesus."

-Helen: "Beautiful family... God bless you for your kindness, it's been days now since my son last bathe... Thanks."

-Mary: "Don't thank me, thank God for His Eternal Mercy, now go... go on and continue cleaning your son".

My mother did cleanse me with the water that Mary used for her Son, then she went to sleep beside her family; afterwards we went to our little tent to sleep.

Next morning, a miracle!... a huge miracle happened, the rash all over me was gone I had a clean skin, my Mother with tears in her eyes thanked God and His Beautiful Mercy because that sickness disappeared all thanks to God and that Mary's baby waters, she always paused when telling the story...

- Helen: "Mary and her son Jesus are blessed... (Sigh)...Mary and Jesus, amazing!"

- Dismas: "Mother... Mother..." (She's day dreaming)

-Helen: "Sorry... well that lady's name was Mary, her husband Joseph and the baby Jesus...if you ever encounter them, please my sweet Dismas... my sweet, sweet, boy Dismas... serve them in any way you can, because I think God favors them, and if you serve them, God will smile on to you."

After years away from our home, my Mother convinced me to leave Egypt with her, I was creating too many problems for her, since we didn't had much, I had to steal every now and then so we could have something to eat. I remember my first masterpiece, I always saw this man coming down from the Hill every morning, he always carried fresh bread to sell, but he always came all the way down sleeping in the top of the mule and with a basket of fresh bread in each side, the mule had a stick with a carrot in front so the mule would follow without problems, each time he came down there was a small part where the mule had to jump a little bit in order for him to wake up, so one day I ran uphill and waited until he passed by me, when he did, as always he was asleep... I took two pieces of fresh bread, I took those every day and he never knew some of his bread was missing.

Once my Mother was really upset with me and she needed to go to the synagogue with my aunt, at the time I was creating to many problems for her, she tied me up in front of the house! I was tied up in front my aunt's house! Couldn't believe what my Mother did! A group of boys saw me tied there, oh! God, here comes trouble... this guys, I never liked them and they didn't like me so they enjoyed themselves kicking and punching me, when my Mother came home, she started crying like I was dying or something, in fact... I was messed a little bit but the thing that hurt me the most was seeing my Mother crying so much, I came into the house clean up a little bit and went to sleep, next morning I got up really early and went out to look for them.

I got one alone outside of his own house, I was so fast that he didn't had the time to call for help, I took out a couple of teeth with my first punch, poor guy he didn't know what was going on, I left him moaning on the ground..., one down three to go! After a while a finally caught up to them, they were outside of town right at the west entrance, I was so angry at them because they made my Mother cry... got there and fill them up with my fists, I got the first in the gut, then the two other guys were paralyze because of the surprise factor, kicked one in groin while the other threw a punch that missed my face but scratched my ear hard, so I punched him in the jaw twice, quickly I turned around and saw the one I got in the gut trying to stand up so I got him in the face with my knee, the one I got in the groin was crying... I was so mad seeing his many tears that it only remind me of my Mother's cry, so I kicked him again there... when all of my energy went south, they were all in the ground.

- Dismas: "If I ever see you guys again I'll tear you apart!"

They slowly started to walk (painfully that is...) away.

- "I'm impressed right know."

- Dismas: "Who are you?"

- "My name is Gestas and I have to say... I'm impressed."

- Dismas: "Well they got what they deserve; I mean... they had it coming because of what they did to me."

- Gestas: "Don't worry, the thing is that you're quick and intelligent, I mean; I've seen what you've been doing to Mr. Roth..."

- Dismas: "Who is Mr. Roth?"

- Gestas: "The one that you've been stealing the breads from."

I was surprised that someone knew what I was doing in that hill, but we both laugh and we quickly became friends as he explained to me that he was like me... a thief, he thought that I was doing an excellent job with Mr. Roth because he never knew what was happening, he told me that he couldn't do that, once he takes something he had to run even if he didn't even need to run, he just had to...and sometimes that hurt him big because by the running the victims knew something was going on.

- Dismas: "The key is to be smooth and let no one know that you were there, for example the other day I was following a lady that had a bag full of apples, as she was walking I got near to her and quickly took three of them, immediately she noticed something was going on so when she turned I said to her "My good lady, this two apples just fell from your bag", she smile to me took one and gave me the other, since I hid one before she even noticed, I got two apples and everybody is happy... she never knew I was a crook."

- Gestas: "Wow... and how old you say you are?"

- Dismas: "Twelve... and you?"

- Gestas: "Fourteen... but that doesn't matter my friend you handle yourself like a man already!"

We laughed hard and a beautiful friendship began, every now and then we got together to create more art, I mean to steal a little bit here and there. We were hated by our rivals, the news about me getting into fights all over town was a growing pain to my Mother, I always told her that I was working in whatever job I could find in town just in case she had any suspicions. Those days were amazing, Gestas and I were enough to take the city and the thing is that nobody ever knew, and if later they knew it was because our rivals always told them that it was us, we always had to fight our competition but they weren't a match for us, we always fought better than they even if they were more.

Since we were at my aunt's house my Mother was attacked verbally every day by my aunt, and it was always because of me... the news by the word from mouth, about what I was doing had her in constant fear, I truly love my Mother so in order to save me from trouble we decided to go to Jerusalem.

Time passed by fast and I was already nineteen years old, Gestas was having fun with Mr. Roth every now and then because we didn't steal his bread anymore, but he liked to mess his schedule up by moving the carrot the mule got around, so the mule could go back up to the hill... I can imagine Mr. Roth's face when he wakes up back where he came from... it was a sad day because me and my Mother had an agreement to go back home, after years living in Egypt.

- Dismas: "Hey thief!, having fun with Mr. Roth again?"

- Gestas: "Yes, it gets funnier every time."

- Dismas: "My friend, I and my Mother came to the agreement to move back to our country."

- Gestas: "I saw that coming my dear friend, you love too much your Mother and all this fighting around town took a toll, so you're leaving all of this?"

- Dismas: "I know you will be fine my friend, sometimes you get a little bit crazy... but you'll do fine without me, I just can't do this to my Mother anymore and besides I'd like to be in the holy city... it has been a dream of mine for long."

- Gestas: "I hope I get to see you again, you piece of dirt."

- Dismas: "God willing I sincerely hope so... peace be with you."

- Gestas: "Peace, thief... peace."

Jerusalem what an awesome city even tough we struggle there for years, I had to do whatever it takes to bring food to our table and it was hard being...Honest! I had to promise my Mother never to steal or fight ever again and that I will trust more our Lord I AM, so... I had to take whatever job that I was offered and most of the time for very little money, my luck started to turn around by my 22nd birthday I got a job cleaning tables at a tavern... my employer was a Judean, a man called Mr. John; he had no family and was very proud to be from Judah, if you ask me I can tell you that he came from hell, he's the worse employer ever, Mr. John always tried to find a way not to spend on salary, he even spitted in some of the meals taken by his clients.

The winter was coming and there was more work but less and less money, that was a little odd because it should've been the contrary with so much work in my hands, the circumstances that took me to my old ways started when Mr. John didn't want to pay me... he showed me three jars with his best wine broken in pieces.

-Mr. John: "Dismas!!!!"..."What happened here, my best wine is gone! You did this on purpose, right? Everything in your life is a joke to you, right? Am I a joke to you; you think I'm a fool...don't you? I'm calling the guards."

- Dismas: "Please wait, I don't know what happened, I know it wasn't me...you have to believe me, please Mr. John".

- Mr. John: "This better be the last time you screw up Dismas, I'm not paying you but on the contrary... you owe me your salary and the next one, and if you even say something... I will call the Romans so that you could go to jail....Back to work!"

It was obvious that it wasn't me, I knew I was the only employee in the tavern at the time, I'm down in my luck... this is so frustrating! I know sometimes there was somebody assisting him with the meals and I believe his name is Isaac...

I think, well even though I don't remember his name but that day it was me and the boss only... This is the boss's doing! He just doesn't want to pay me! Mr. John thinks he's clever enough to steal from me, but he doesn't know that I'm the original thief out of Egypt; well, because of my Mother... the original retired Thief out of Egypt.

Next day Mr. John needed to go to the Temple to pray, yeah right...Mr. John always went to the Temple, so he could be seen giving money as offerings he liked people to think he was great, he always closed at a certain time, always sending the cook to the market even for nothing and left me with all the work, one day I had a break... cleaning up the tavern at my own pace, I did my job properly always preparing for the upcoming clients and their potential tips, all of the sudden, the door bang loudly...

Bang, bang, bang.

The Romans? The Romans were at the door!

-"Open up, we need to celebrate, open now!!"

So I opened the door and put a smile on my face even though I wanted to spit in their beastly faces!!

- Dismas: "Please come in."

The place got filled with a troop of romans and they wanted wine, lots of it...!! I started to give them service, so many drinks passed by and in little time they were all drunk, some of them payed for the wine, some were so confuse that they mistakenly gave me more money, and others they didn't' even pay; after a while they all went their ways singing a foreign chant, I had a small fortune in my hands, so quickly I went to the back and buried all the money, it was 304 denarii so I left out 4 denarii for my beloved Mr. John.

When Mr. John came back, he looked in disbelief with all the mess left behind by the Romans...

- Mr. John: "What happened here...! It's all upside down! What happened Dismas!!!?"

- Dismas: "While you were gone, a troop of Romans came by and I couldn't stay closed for them, I feared for my life... so they came in and started to drink, they drank almost all the wine we had in storage, they didn't want any food...only wine, they left only 4 denarii and went away all drunk".

- Mr. John: "4 Denarii?... 4 denarii? But that can't be!! They drank more than a 300 denarii worth of wine!!! 4 denarii?... Oh I'm ruined!

Oh! Yes he was, the thing is that the wine wasn't even paid yet to the wine provider, so it wasn't just going to be a 300 denarii hole, but most likely the provider would file a claim and Mr. John would find himself in trouble with his reputation tarnished... I was loving it!! As a matter of fact I didn't care he deserves it; I was underpaid, abused, and tricked out of my salary numerous times so I say justice was served.

-SLAP!!-

- Dismas: "Now why did you hit me now?"...

- Mr. John: "It's your entire fault!... You ruined me, boy!... I don't care if they would have killed you... You should've stay closed! Why did you open the door for them?"

- Dismas: "Now how could it be that I'm at fault? You know that no one can stop the Romans, you know this! If the door would have remained closed then what next? They would have torn it apart!"

- Mr. John: "I don't care!! I don't care if it would have meant your pathetic life, you're a fool...you're nothing but dirt, Dismas you're fired...I don't want to see you ever again ...you worthless bastard!"

At that point I wasn't thinking, quickly I took a big piece of wood lying on the ground... didn't even know why and how it got there; I first hit him in the legs, he fell down awkwardly.

- Dismas: "No one calls me a bastard!, and I'm glad that you are ruined!".

I hit him twice, one in the left arm and the other one in the chest...I made him beg for his life.

- Mr. John: "Oh, please...please, I'm sorry Dismas... have mercy".

- Dismas: "Yeap, I am sorry I didn't do this much sooner... goodbye Mr. John."

After a couple of more swings I kicked him in the face and he went out cold, I took some of the goods, money that was buried and before the cook comes in, I left!

Quickly I went to the Holy Temple were my mother likes to be at times, she likes it there... praying into boredom, I don't know how someone could do that! When I found her I told her that I messed up in my Job, I told her that Mr. John and I had a fight then she got scared because of my reckless past, for her this time could be the one to take my life away.

-Helen: "You promised! You promised son!!"

- Dismas: "Yes, I know Mother...it's just... my abusive employer got me mad and... well it doesn't matter I'm in trouble so we need to go Mother, now!"

We took the road out of Jerusalem we were headed to our old house in Bethlehem; since I've never told anybody that we were from Bethlehem, instead, that we came from Egypt... I was in hope for a good disappearance act, I thought: if we went to Egypt eventually that's where they will pursue me, there... I could get caught eventually. Misleading everybody was a good thing hoping for the best and a new beginning, my Mother spent the whole day of travel like always...

talking about my father, how much I looked like him, that I need a wife, worried about my future, always telling me the same stories and always finishing crying.

- Dismas: "Mother don't cry, please... try and understand that now your husband is with God, let's look ahead for a new day."

-Helen: "Thanks my sweet Dismas, I know that he is in heaven and it is my hope that almighty God calls me to be up there soon so I could be with God and him... please Almighty One take me soon, please take me swiftly, make haste I AM, find a good wife for my Dismas so he wouldn't be alone in the world... I need to be gone for good my God, You are I AM all Merciful and Beautiful, please take me soon."

- Dismas: "Don't talk like that Mother and let's focus on this trip."

-Helen: "..."

For almost half a day we had to walk to Bethlehem, our native town, when we got there I was missing Jerusalem already, Bethlehem was an ugly and small town, thank God that we still had our little house...it was a little bit messy and needed much work to be done here, but I wasn't afraid of work. It was the beginning of winter, I figured that there wasn't any jobs... but I didn't care I had a 300 denarii to my disposal, I quickly got food and some goods, when I returned to the house I found out that an uncle I've never knew was there.

- Helen: "Dismas this is Benjamin, your uncle... He is the brother of you father Simon."

- Benjamin: "It is so good to see you both, we heard that you guys took the path to Egypt to save your lives, it is so good to see you."

- Helen: "Likewise, Benjamin... it is a blessing to see you again."

- Dismas: "Well, please to meet you Benjamin, I'm sure that you'll stay for a little meal...won't you?"

- Benjamin: "I'm sorry, I can't now I'm in a hurry, but you need to come to my house...you will be my guests of honor...please come."

- Helen: "I must apologize but I don't feel too well from all this traveling, if you want Dismas you could go yourself right now, I need to sleep a little bit."

- Dismas: "Sure Mother... I accept your invitation Benjamin."

- Dismas: "I'll catch you later Benjamin, I'll be there soon."

- Benjamin: "Please call me Uncle Ben... I'll be waiting."

My Mother after Benjamin left was crying silently, so I asked her what was going on and why she didn't mention him to me... and she said:

-Helen: "Unfortunately we have no other family than this one right here, Benjamin never helped us while we were away, never even bother to know how his nephew was; after his brother got killed by the Romans, the only thing that matter to him was everything but us... he sent someone to Egypt telling me that he wanted to get this house from us, back then I said that it was my son's house now and when you get older by that time you'll decide, this house isn't much but it was left by your grandfather to your father, I really don't understand why he wants it so bad! Your father didn't want me to worry with all his family troubles, so please don't be surprise if tonight he asks you this house away from you."

- Dismas: "Don't worry I won't sell it, I know this house is where you and father used to live and I think that you still cherish that."

- Helen: "Even though we had this house and we struggled in Jerusalem I didn't want to come until you were ready, I knew how much you wanted to be in the Holy City."

- Dismas: "Yes Mother I used to love Jerusalem, but don't you worry; now let me get clean up, yes...?"

- Helen: "Yes…"

I went out, took some water from the well and took me only a few minutes to get clean, when I was done I got dressed quickly, came out and saw my mother with a tear in her eyes remembering when I got healed by the water that used that lady from the desert to bathe her son.

- Helen: "I know that I have told you a hundred times that story as we were fleeing from the Romans, but it gives me great joy and happiness knowing that you got cured from that horrible disease my sweet boy, I wonder what happened to that family."

- Dismas: "What was the name of that lady and her son again?"

- Helen: "Mary and Jesus."

- Dismas: "Oh yes…yes, well… I'll be back soon Mother."

-Helen: "Yes my son be careful out there…you're all I have left in this world my son, take care."

I went out to my uncle's house with the thought of what he really wants and why. He never tried to know how we were or how the only son of his brother is; I got there fairly quickly walking from my house and introduced myself to his family.

- Benjamin: "Peace be with you my boy… this is my wife Keila and my son Jairo please come in,we were waiting for you"

- Dismas: "Peace to you all…please to meet you, my name is Dismas."

We quickly sat down and Benjamin didn't even pray the customary thanks to God for the food in the table, I know I'm a crook myself but at least one with principle.

- Dismas: "Benjamin I must admit that I'm impressed, this is a good house in this little town for a Sheepherder."

- Benjamin: "Well sheep didn't cut that much for me nephew, I had to star lending a little bit of money here... a little bit of money there, I started very small but now I'm quite successful... but anyways I'm happy that you guys are back...it's unfortunate about your father, my brother... to this day we don't know what the Romans did with his body; but anyways I want to talk to you about an agreement your father and I had for me to acquire your house, now that your back we could get that agreement again."

- Dismas: "No, Mother told me that you and my father didn't see eye to eye because my grandfather left the house to him before he died, so I don't know why you're saying that you and Father had an agreement when I know for fact that's not true."

- Benjamin: "Look, you didn't even were born when our Father gave that House to my little brother, he knew that I was his firstborn, but forget it! I have a proposition for you... I'll give you a farm in the outside of Bethlehem and 40 denarii so you could start your own sheep thing or whatever you like to do."

- Dismas: "I apologize Benjamin but the house of my father is not for sale, anyways with 40 denarii I couldn't buy the door of house! Since I'm the only son I can provide for my Mother, so thanks...but no thanks, good night!"

-Benjamin: "Boy, don't you walk away from me...you'll regret this, come back I tell you!"

Couldn't stay, for him I wasn't view as family but as an obstacle needed to be overcome, that's why I never asked him about why he never wanted to get to know his nephew, well I'll have to start a business or something now that we are in Bethlehem... but what? Forgive me father but being a sheepherder or working the land is not for me, I'll just have to be creative...what it'll be? What it'll be?... A tavern!, that's it...a tavern!

A tavern was started in my own house (thank you Mr. John for the money!)... It was a little tavern and the only one in town... so business was fair, provided me and my mother most of the time.

Ten years passed by since I got to Bethlehem, we weren't rich or anything but we were happy, thank God that nothing from Jerusalem followed us here! Though... I always wondered what I left behind with Mr. John after all that beating... Nah! I couldn't care less, even though Jerusalem was near Bethlehem no news from Jerusalem ever came after me.

During the winter my mother got sick... very sick, she wasn't the same person anymore, like I used to know: energetic woman, lots of life, sweet and caring Mother... Her sickness started little, even though she took remedies her illness never wanted to go away, on a shiny and beautiful day she got worst, she fainted in the back of our house cleaning some fish to eat, I put her on her bed, I closed the tavern and told her that I needed her more than ever, please don't leave me Mother! I was shocked to see she was giving up on life, like she wanted death to happen, I paid doctors and more doctors taking our finances downhill and nothing seemed to cure her, it's been one hell of a week... I didn't know what to do anymore and on a Tuesday afternoon she gave me her final words.

- Helen: (It was hard for her to speak)"You don't need me anymore Dismas........ You need God and I need to be with your father....... I love you very much....... I have loved you .... all of my life......... I've been waiting this.......I long to be with your father....... within the Mercy of God....... try and live well....... under the eyes....... of I AM....... so we could..... see...... you...... again in para....di...sss....ee...(sigh).

- Dismas: (Crying) "Mother! Mother!, Mother!!"

I mourned for months, the tavern was sometimes open some other days closed, I couldn't handle it anymore, so I had the tavern closed for good, until I could get my head straight and this pain of my chest.... One day walking out of Bethlehem I started hearing somebody's laughter...

- Ha, ha, ha, ha, ha...

- Look around Dismas, do you see a familiar face?

- Dismas: "Jairo?"

- Jairo: "Yes, cousin…is me Jairo, I just can't help it… you're so funny."

Jairo was all grown up, how times passes so quickly… he was with two of his friends beneath a tree and they were all laughing.

- Dismas: "What is so funny Jairo, please… you know what? I don't want to know… right now I don't have time for you; don't you know that I'm mourning?"

- Jairo: "Oh yes I know that you are, it's just ironic how life treats you…bastard one day and whor…umm!! Motherless the next."

I think that he was saying something to his friends about the house of my grandfather, that it was theirs and after that I didn't hear nothing more, everything was blah, blah, blah, blah to me as I jumped him and his friends with my fists; my inner fire took over, the one I used in Egypt decades ago took control as I fought three men, didn't stop until knocking them all until I was covered in their blood, they were all moaning, crying and in pain… after that I just ran away for a good while.

Got out of Bethlehem without thinking what I just did, all I could think was that I was alone in the world, alone in the world! Didn't have a wife, family or children… I know I never got the opportunity anyway, my father and my mother dead, I'm all alone! A few days later I realized that I was near the city of Jericho, guess I walked a great distance without giving too much of a thought were I was going! All dirty with no money, as I was entering Jericho the hunger for food was big, I was desperate… so I put my skills to the test… quickly I took two pieces of bread from a vendor in the streets without she ever knowing who took it, I'm still good at this! Sorry Mother, as I was walking away from the center of the town to the outside, I knew I need to get back to Bethlehem soon.

Suddenly I heard:

-There you are you little piece of dirt…!

Smack!

Some people came to me out of nowhere and started punching me with sticks, beating me up like I was some kind of a criminal…wait! On second thought I am a criminal; guess somebody saw me after all, the last thing I remember before somebody knocked me unconscious was:

- Thief…thief!

They left me up for dead in the middle of the road, I don't know for how long I was out, somebody told me later that many people passed me by like nothing happened, nobody did anything for me…nobody; but a man from Samaria took me to an inn, after he cleaned my wounds and took care of me, paid 20 denarii instructing them to continue my care until he returns, and whatever difference in money when he comes back will be paid by him. If you ask me, that's a big waste of money and for a total stranger, but I have to admit that I needed that so badly, nobody besides my Mother ever took care of me like that before, I was way sore but at the same time intrigued by such a nice gesture.

A week passed by in this inn right outside of Jericho, I was still waiting for the Samaritan to show up, my healing process was quick all thanks to I AM and this strange Samaritan, I needed to give thanks and tell him that I'll promise to give back his money, after two weeks recovering from my injuries The Samaritan finally arrived.

- How are you my friend? How everybody has treated you here?

- Dismas: "I'm better thanks to you.

- "Nice… Nice…"

- Dismas : "Now… Why did you help me?… Who are you?"

- "I saw someone in need and I felt compassionate, in my mind I saw someone that I already have seen before, the only time I saw Him... He was radiant and only in need for one's heart for God, He was teaching in the top of a Hill, teaching anybody that would want to listen, His words got stuck in me... though I was far from Him, His words traveled easily and came down on me like thunder, resonated throughout my entire soul!"

- Dismas: "What words?"

- He said:

"Blessed are the poor in spirit, for theirs is the kingdom of heaven."

"Blessed are they who mourn, for they will be comforted."

"Blessed are the meek, for they will inherit the land."

"Blessed are they who hunger and thirst for righteousness, for they will be satisfied."

"Blessed are the merciful, for they will be shown mercy."

"Blessed are the clean of heart, for they will see God."

"Blessed are the peacemakers, for they will be called children of God."

"Blessed are they who are persecuted for the sake of righteousness, for theirs is the kingdom of heaven."

"Blessed are you when they insult you and persecute you and utter every kind of evil against you (falsely) because of me. Rejoice and be glad, for your reward will be great in heaven."

"Thus they persecuted the prophets who were before you. You are the salt of the earth. But if salt loses its taste, with what can it be seasoned? It is no longer good for anything but to be thrown out and trampled underfoot."

"You are the light of the world. A city set on a mountain cannot be hidden. Nor do they light a lamp and then put it under a bushel basket; it is set on a lampstand, where it gives light to all in the house just so, your light must shine before others, that they may see your good deeds and glorify your heavenly Father."

- "Those words still are inside me like my very blood... I wanted to go to Him, I wanted to ask a few questions but the crowd kept me away from where He was. I kept repeating these words and wanted to live by them, I kept thinking that I shall receive Mercy if I'm merciful, but how can I be merciful if don't know the true meaning of Mercy?... suddenly walking out from Jericho to Bethsaida there you were my friend... my mind played tricks on me because I wasn't seeing you, I was seeing Him! I was shocked to see it was Him...

Even though Jews and Samaritans don't get along, despite our differences my soul had a strong desire to assist Him, I just couldn't help it! I was driven to serve Him... Then finally I understood! That the desire to help Him was an epiphany from God... God himself sprinkles the rain over good and bad, that action God takes is Mercy! So I was given this knowledge: Mercy is the arms and legs of true Love, these arms and legs they act on all of us for our good, so if I become an extension of that Mercy, my wonderful God in Heaven would give me Mercy someday, by letting me live past this life with Him forever! As He said: "Blessed are the merciful, for they will be shown mercy."

Now after that epiphany... I didn't saw Him anymore, I just saw you... I did my very best to try take care of your wounds, I know what I saw and I know this is right, I tell you the truth I'll pray that I can continue to do this type of work throughout my entire life... Please my brother don't think that I am crazy, His words change me forever and I want to live my life being merciful so that my Father up in Heaven gives me Mercy, I know He will if I persevere being His arms and legs down here."

- Dismas: "No... you're not crazy! But wait... who was this person? And what is your name?"

The Samaritan walked towards the owner of the inn, gave him 20 denarii more for their troubles, walked to the door and before my lips could even say something, his final words were:

- "My friend don't worry about my name, I'm just somebody that loves God, somebody giving out Mercy for the sake of God, the name of the man that said the words I referred a while back to you, is Jesus...if you ever see Him... follow Him you will not be disappointed, get well my friend...peace be with you."

The Samaritan walked away from my life in a hurry!! didn't even had the chance to thank him properly, though I was still feeling sore from my injuries and still couldn't get over Helen's death, I went back home, the people at that inn were nice enough to give me food and water for the road, I joined a caravan going to Bethsaida since Bethlehem is near that town I was happy to go.

During the journey I encounter an old pal, an old friend of mine within the caravan...

- Dismas: "Gestas...?

- Dismas: "Gestas! I salute the... thief of Egypt..."

- Gestas: "It cannot be! My old friend Dismas! How are things, what news you have?"

- Dismas: "Nothing from the old life, you know... my Mother made me quit the life."

- Gestas: "I'm sorry but nobody ever can tell me to stop...this is me, this who I am and I Love it!"

Gestas my partner in crime in Egypt, we used to do some stealing here and there since we were kids and we never got caught, but one thing I always disliked about him, is that he was sometimes dumb and wild at times, I always liked to think before any job; I heard by the word of the mouth by a relative of him, that after we got to Jerusalem he killed somebody during a robbery. For me was out of the question to kill for a steal, I'm the type of thief (well, used to be), that for me it was some sort of art, like making tricks as a magician... now you see it now you don't, nobody ever knew it was me!

Even though we never got caught sometimes we ran into trouble with the authority, sometimes with people and sometimes with rivals, and mostly it was because of him... killing people was just insane.

We talked for hours about things we did in Egypt, all that happened with me and my Mother in Jerusalem, he told me that he needed to flee the Old city because of a bad situation with a few rivals and ended up in Jericho, it was like old times remembering the past and all, joking here and there... then we got interrupted by two men passing us by.

- "Yes! My friend, that was beautiful, this Jesus is awesome! He can cure anything... and even I heard that he can throw out demons from possessed people."

- "Really? That is amazing! I would like to see Him, I want to see his next trick."

- "No fool, that's no trick...the guy is a prophet for real, He cures people, He throws out demons, He even blessed some waters at a wedding and people say the waters turned into wine, He is the real thing and He teaches the people with wonderful wisdom."

- Dismas: "Excuse me, what name did you say that guy you mentioned was...?"

- "Jesus."

- Dismas: "Well...and you were saying that he cures people and say nice things?"

- "Yes."

- Dismas: "What exactly does He say?"

- Well I saw Him once... He was speaking to thousands of people, He said something like: "Blessed are they that mourn for they shall be comforted", "Blessed are the merciful for they shall receive mercy" and so many other things, but those are the only ones I remember."

- Dismas: "I have heard that before, it is Jesus indeed."

- Gestas: "If you ask me, that's just a total waste of time."

- Dismas: "My Mother use to tell me something about some guy named Jesus and His Mother Mary, my Mother use to tell me about a miracle given to us through them..."

- Gestas: "Really?"

- Dismas: "Yes... I was sick and got healed with the waters that the Mother of Jesus used for Him as a baby."

- "Well that is awesome (The stranger replied), He walks with many people including some women, I don't know if His Mother is called Mary."

- Dismas: "That's fine; well thank you for those news..."

- Gestas: "Yeah thanks for the interruption."

As they walk away with a weird look in their eyes because of what Gestas said, I wondered what an amazing story came to us and what a coincidence.

- Gestas: "Hey...come back to earth Dismas... come back..."

- Dismas: "Sorry... It's been rough for me lately; I lost my Mother three weeks ago... I almost killed a guy in Bethlehem... and finally in Jericho somebody kicked my behind pretty bad."

- Gestas: "Really! Back in Egypt nobody could beat you, not even me!"

- Dismas: "Well they got me off guard... but a good person took care of me while I was down, my wounds got better because of I AM first and that guy, but regarding that beating... there was too many people at once so they just won the fight..."

We talked for hours about things that we did in the past, things that were fun back then, right now Gestas was the only person in the world that I knew I could count on; Gestas became the only friend I had in the world. We got to Bethsaida and it has been weeks since that incident with Jairo took place, I hope that I could just start over and we could forget everything that happened, I'm not in the mood to fight again.

Walking through the road I saw an old client of my tavern...

- Dismas: "Hey Mr. Seth, how are you? You are very far from Bethlehem; please do know that I will open my tavern soon for all my good customers."

- Seth: "Hello... what? You didn't know?"

- Dismas: "???"

- Seth: "The tavern got into a fire... everybody in town worked to put the fire out, but it consumed everything."

- Dismas: "What? Uncle Ben, it had to be him! It was revenge for his son Jairo."

- Seth: "Jairo, is actually looking for you all around so they could accuse you for his beating, they tried to do it while you were gone but the accusation didn't bear fruit because you weren't present."

- Dismas: "I thank you much for this information Mr. Seth."

- Seth: "Be well Dismas, and please take this humble advice... try to settle somewhere else, it is not worth it to get involved in more trouble, peace be with you...."

- Dismas: "Peace..."

- Gestas: "If you are going to do something my friend... count me in."

- Dismas: "I guess that I'll do nothing... I'm tired; need to go somewhere they can't find me, I know that in time they'll think that I will never come back and just leave everything to rest."

- Gestas: "Look... if I were you, I just wait for good time to attack them... if they're dead, their accusations will never surface, sometimes you think they'll forget... but it's the contrary."

- Dismas: "No, Gestas... I was never a murderer, just a thief... even though what you say is true, my Mother wouldn't approve it if she were alive, killing is not what I am...so no...that's out of the question."

- Gestas: "Well, if you want I'll do it for you..."

- Dismas: "NO!!!... Gestas no, since when you kill people my friend...? I tell you leave it in peace."

- Gestas: "Sorry... it's just that, sometimes when you're cornered you do it, and once you pass that line... it becomes easy to do it again."

- Dismas: "Well I'm sorry Gestas, please... leave it in peace."

We didn't spend much time in Bethsaida, another caravan was set to go to Egypt, we went with them mostly because they were going to pass by Bethlehem, I wanted to see my house for the last time. We got there at night, I needed to stay quiet in my tent away from it all, I'll check at dawn before the caravan starts to head to Jerusalem... Gestas wanted to go out; he said that he needed to see the town a little bit.

- Gestas: "I'm going out my friend; I'm going to see your little town."

- Dismas: "Please my friend, go to my house and check everything there, so you could tell me in the morning, try not to get in trouble... and please try not to mess things for me."

- Gestas: "More than they are my friend? Sure I'll do it."

I gave him some directions about where my house was, then I went to sleep and a little later, what do you know? That turned out to be my biggest mistake ever!! Gestas came in later talking and breathing heavily.

- Gestas: "Now you have no more problems my friend, don't now get soft on me...Ha,ha,ha,ha now you don't have any enemies, Ha,ha,ha,ha."

- Dismas: "What are you talking about fool, I need my sleep... what is it?"

- Gestas: "I went out on the town to check out you know, I went to the place you told me and yes it was in ruins... all burned, but all of the sudden a couple of guys came to the ruins, since I was inside the burned home I hid, they didn't see me and they were speaking to themselves."

- Benjamin: "He's not family anymore, after what he did to you Jairo...if Dismas shows his face I will personally strangled the life out of him with my own hands! I put up with him all of these years, I struggled with the thought about killing him and that whore as well, but now the whore is gone and he tried to kill you... Even if it takes a lifetime I will find him and kill him."

- Jairo: "So what shall we do about this ruins?"

- Benjamin: "Go and find your friends, they're good workers...you know that they could use the pay, even though I know I can't use this property for nothing more than storage, it's worth it... finally I have the house that it was supposed to be mine from the beginning, my mother wanted me to have it, but it was my father's decision to give it to Simon."

- Benjamin: "We always had a bad relationship because he was always the preferred one in the eyes of our father, for everything I always had to give way, give way, give way because he was the preferred son... well enough of that nonsense already, Simon is dead and his son should be soon; now go and tell your friends that work is needed... go!"

- Gestas: "As the boy departed from the old man, I was still hidden in the back when a part where I was hiding surrender to my weight and broke into little pieces... I should have known better."

- Benjamin: "Who is there...? Answer me, damn it."

- Gestas: "Ha, ha, ha, ha, ha... old man today is your lucky night, but also will be the lucky night of my friend...Dismas."

- Benjamin: "I don't want any trouble, but if you come near I'll stick this knife in your gut!"

- Gestas: "Please... I will take your knife and rip you into pieces with it, before you're dead you will see your gut all over the floor old man."

- Benjamin: "Please don't, I'll give you money just walk away."

- Gestas: "Old man I'll take that money from you and kill you also, unfortunately for you I'm loyal to my friends, and before Dismas is dead I prefer that you be dead a thousand times more."

- Gestas: "The old man threw the knife at me, I stopped the knife in midair while he was trying to escape, he stumbled in his retreat and took the opportunity and stab him in the back multiple times, he started crying and shouting like the coward he truly is.

-Benjamin: "Jairo, Jairo, someone help!! Please, they are killing me help... Dismas and his friend!!"

- Gestas: "I was in shock, he didn't knew my name but started shouting your name instead, that was weird... anyways after a while his voice started to dim down, as the life started to go away from the man, I took his money bag and came here... don't get soft on me Dismas, I wasn't looking for that, it just fell on my lap... look we have 70 denarii in this bag."

- Dismas: (Speechless).

- Gestas: "you're not saying anything Dismas, I just gave you a gift... I just got rid of your biggest enemy...well, say something Dismas!"

- Dismas: "Gestas you fool, you didn't gave me a gift... you gave me a curse, you killed my uncle and I didn't want him dead, also because he shouted my name the surrounding neighbors will think that I was the one who did it, my uncle was respected in town, everybody knew him and I guess that everybody knew our rift...I know we didn't see eye to eye, but I stayed years here in Bethlehem without him harassing me at all even though he could, he left me and my Mother to live and work in peace, I guess that he eventually realized that me and my Mother didn't have anything to do with whatever happened between his father, my father and him."

- Gestas: "But Dismas he was telling this other guy that he wanted you dead! Come on now don't get soft on me, what is done is done and besides look at all this money!"

- Dismas: "Keep it... I don't want any of it, now I have to run my stupid friend because of you I'm going to run... if I were you I'll do the same because they saw you with me in this caravan, it'll be soon rather than later that they will come here to get us, so let's go!"

- Gestas: "You're right... let's go."

It seems that I have been running all my life, this time I wasn't looking for trouble but trouble came down looking for me, sometimes that's the life of a thief... we usually give problems to everybody, but sometimes even bigger problems come knocking at our doors, it's ironic because I did left this type of path, but trouble came anyway.

In Jericho I stole a couple of breads for the first time in a decade and I got punished for it, I wanted to go back to a normal life and all it took was an old friend from my previous criminal life to mess it all up, life is unfair even for an ex-thief like me...

So, this is what happened to me for being a thief... even though I was practically out, my friend ruined it for me, and the worst part is that I can't go anywhere for help because I don't have anybody but myself. They'll check our caravan right away so we had to fled immediately to Jerusalem, since Jairo knew that I lived in Egypt most of my life, I figured that he'll go there first; we got to the Holy city, needed to stay quiet for a few weeks, Gestas had a place here in Jerusalem (actually it was more of a rat hole than a house) and stayed there for a while.

I still had my Mother in my mind, thinking of her every night and always with questions in my head, "what if", "what if"... I was sleeping one night and I had this dream: I was walking through the desert's sand when heard somebody crying from a far distance, I started running towards the sound of the cry, the sound kept getting bigger and bigger until I finally got to a small tent, I stopped and saw my Mother inside watching something or someone lying in the ground, I said: "Why are you crying Mother" but she didn't replied, I tried to touch her in her shoulder but my hand went right through her, she was crying even harder...inconsolably, I couldn't see what she was seeing in the ground so I turned to get a better view... the shock to know that... it was me!, rotten all the way... me! A leper! Putridity I saw everywhere, I was almost dead because of this leprosy! I woke up in a sea of my own sweat.

- Gestas: "Dismas are you alright..?

- Dismas: "Yes... it was just a dream."

-Gestas: "Dismas my friend I have to tell to you that It's been almost half a year since we ran from Bethlehem, you need to start some jobs here and there... you can't be like this forever!"

- Dismas: "Yes, your right my friend I need to start something... what do you have in mind?"

- Gestas: "I'm sure that we could find something of value out there to steal... are you up for it? Do you remember how to do it?"

- Dismas: "Please, you'll see the master in action."

- Gestas: "What master? The one from Egypt or the one that got beat in Jericho?"

We both started laughing and we went out, we were like those kids in Egypt again... nobody ever knew that we were stealing until much later when we were already gone, at the end of the day we were a success in Jerusalem, when we got to the rat hole we had a small fortune between us...well a very small fortune, in total we had 30 denarii, bread from the temple, four jars of wine, even a Roman sword! For this sword we'll get good money; yes it was good times all over again.

Time passed by and I was about to get my 35th birthday in a few months, walking near the old tavern where I used to work; nobody there that I knew back in the day, in fact it was administer by somebody else, I guess those 300 denarii was too much for Mr. John, well why do I even care! It's been like forever seen last I saw him, all covered in his own blood... that though came to me like if it was yesterday, but funny thing is that I had an overwhelming feeling of regret, I tried to shake it off but couldn't for a while, until in front of me passed by the most beautiful eyes I have ever seen... ever!! I was captivated by so much beauty, I had to know who she was... she isn't royalty... she was definitely Jewish.

Suddenly a commotion coming our way near the entrance to Jerusalem caught my attention, they were all shouting:

-"Hosanna to the Son of David; blessed is He who comes in the name of the Lord; hosanna in the highest."

Many people receiving this person, some put their cloaks and branches from the trees on the road... he was passing mounted in a donkey and some people asked:

- "Who is this?"

- They replied: "this is Jesus the prophet from Nazareth, Galilee."

It was way too many people behind Him so I couldn't follow the girl of my dreams, she got away! There goes my luck again... she's gone! But then I saw The Prophet directly from the side... Tall man, beard, with a peaceful expression in His face, he did have a large entourage with Him, men and women... I was laughing because a man was trying to stop His entire entourage and told Jesus to make all the people quiet.

- "Teacher, rebuke your disciples."

- Jesus: "I tell you, if they keep silent, the stones will cry out!"

He did this with authority and He had sort of an edge, the type of person that was able to block nonsense and at the same time He gave peace only with a look, I've never seen somebody ever giving so much peace, this Jesus seems to me more than meets the eye... I wanted to follow where He was going, but too many people were blocking me so I headed back to Gesta's rat hole and called it a day.

The night came pretty quick and I kept all day thinking about this girl, I was imagining a life with her away from all the trouble and all persecution...

I guess that's why time passed me by pretty quick, just because of the sweet thought of having her, I fell asleep and again got the same dream... running in the desert getting to Mother while she was crying and seeing me crumbling into pieces, rotting in front of my Mother's very eyes... I couldn't escape the dream sometimes, seeing myself in such a putrid state...even the smell was there in my nose creating in my insides a nauseous feeling... again waking up again in a sea of my sweat, sometimes that dream repeated itself throughout the night, waking up and seeing beside me that putrid me...horrendous!

It was morning already and I couldn't continue to sleep, Gestas was somewhere in town since last night, he was enjoying himself, drinking and being with prostitutes that was him alright.

I stayed the whole morning thinking about those eyes, will I see them again? Maybe and what can I do to make her mine?...how can I change my luck for the better? Can I change in order to avoid chaos? Will I have the strength to change? Can I change? I have little money, I'm wanted out there and if I'm caught the future will be no longer, for me... Marriage...? What can I give to anybody out there? Nothing but trouble! I was deeply sad within my soul all morning; later something came to me that gave me peace... what the Samaritan did for me.

In an instant I remembered every word that the Samaritan said to me and he looked happy, he seemed like walking on air....some people believes that all Samaritans are heretic because they worship God in mount Gerizim instead of the Holy Temple, they are called among themselves the guardians of the Law, I don't know about that but to me they're alright, this Samaritan follows Jesus the prophet, most likely this has cast himself out from his peers... I remember that some were saying that he is the son of King David... what if this was true? What if he is truly King David's son?

The people are divided over Him, some Jews hate him and others love Him to death. The words of the Samaritan were pounding in my heart and in my soul, "Blessed are the merciful, for they will be shown mercy." The Samaritan was Merciful so he could receive mercy; if I am Merciful then Mercy shall I receive? A little light went on in my soul because I desperately need Mercy in my life, so I went to the Holy Temple... since I'm not worthy to even be around the Temple I started to pray in a corner a couple of houses away from it, but I didn't stand a chance against those beautiful eyes, which interrupted my prayers right in the middle of it, she was walking from the temple... talking to a priest which gave her a blessing and send her away with Temple guards, so this time I had to follow her, maybe my luck finally is changing. She is very young... very young and beautiful indeed, she stopped to get some groceries on the way and some beggars caught the attention of the guards, I tried to get near her... suddenly some woman nearby whispered to her:

- "Psst! Miriam... Miriam... over here... over here."

Then she started running towards that woman, I followed suit as the guards lost her... I guess it was her intention all the way, she went to the outside of town to check the country side, she was so happy... I imagine myself with her and a couple of boys around us dancing with nature, watching life goes by, no troubles, no problems, only love... love. Oh Mother how happy is this thought! It would had make you happy I'm sure, then something was wrong... a couple of guys came and attacked the two women looking for money I believe; I ran like there's no tomorrow... they had her on the ground and she was crying hard.

- "You better give me something of value right now or else."

That was all I was able to hear when I jumped on the guy broke his nose with my very first punch, the other try to hit me with a stick and missed, luckily momentum brought me down to the ground, quickly I rolled into his legs and then he fell on his back, I gave him a big one in the stomach while on the ground, that's when the one that got his nose broken started kicking me in my side, the guards came down running and the two criminals fled the fight running downhill fast, when I was about to flee... the guards caught me.

With spears around my neck there was nothing much that I could do, anyways the two girls were in shock so they couldn't explain right away what happened, I went to some place beside the Holy Temple, I was there the whole afternoon until somebody came and spoke to me.

- "The girl you just saved is my daughter and I want to thank you, I apologize for the behavior of the guards, as you have seen my daughter have told me everything, please...what is your name?"

- Dismas: "My name is Dismas."

- "Well, well, Dismas... Greek for sunshine... my name is Yeshua, Dismas... please I need to know, how can I pay your good deed today?"

- Dismas: "A good deed is a good deed only to be paid by God, so I'm only wishing His Sweet Mercy upon me, you don't have to give me anything."

- Yeshua: "Well said... but please I'll try to accommodate whatever is that you want, please tell me."

- Dismas: "I don't need material things, so the only thing....no forget it, it's just crazy... I'm getting old at 35 and you wouldn't want to know what just came to my mind."

- Yeshua: "Please, I must know."

In my mind I was tired of the life that I was having, tired of all my misfortunes and wanting something better for myself, this guy was giving me some type of a cushion, I was getting anxious to tell Him from the top of my lungs that I was in love with his daughter, but Yeshua seemed someone of high importance, so maybe would be a bad thing to tell the truth here.

- Yeshua: "Please, I must know."

- Dismas: "I want your permission to speak to you daughter in a friendly manner, to see if I could get to know her and Miriam could get to know me."

His whole face change from being so sweet with me to a face in shock, then out of nothing a big laughter came out…

- Yeshua: "Ha, ha, ha, ha, ha… You're right Dismas, it's crazy… look you little piece of dirt, because you saved her and her friend I will not tell my father… the High Priest Caifas, that you wanted for yourself his precious granddaughter, I will let you go Dismas you shall have Mercy today, that's exactly what you are seeking from God… but if I ever know that you're near of my daughter, I will have you arrested…what is it that you are thinking? It is obvious that you are a low class man, you have no family of great importance because nobody around here knows you, so I thank you greatly for saving her but I don't ever want to see you again…Guards!!"

My luck has failed me again; I took a chance and failed miserably, Yeshua is a priest and his father is the high priest! I have put the entire priest clan in my list of enemies who wants to kill me, my mind is about to burn down in flames as the guards threw me out on the road, I think I stayed there on the ground for a while, people passed by and they didn't care… to say the truth I didn't want them to…

Slowly I began to walk away, a tear came dropping from my eyes and more tears started to come down silently, even though Yeshua was right to act like he did because I was a nobody, I was hoping that I could reach my daydream fantasy, instead my life with her went away with all the children that we both could have had, one thought came to my mind...

"Blessed are they who mourn, for they will be comforted."

Jesus... Jesus said those words and right now I need some comfort, more than ever; The prophet might have something from God in those words, I need to be happy again, happy as I was when my sweet Mother was alive, I'm tired of the same thing every day, I'm alone with this feelings... Alone in the world! The same every day with a big hole in my heart, I'm tire of everything that has brought me only disillusion, suffering and tears... I was walking towards the outside of town, beneath a tree I kneel and from the top of lungs I cried:

- Dismas: "I AM...my God, Almighty Creator... (crying), I'm sorry for my sins, promised you from this day forward never to sin again, it doesn't matter how hard it will be from now on, I want to be happy again, PLEASE HEAR ME my SWEET, SWEET GOD... I want to be yours, please show me the way..."

I stayed there on the ground crying for long, I was so tired from everything and anything... without knowing, I went to sleep and went back to the same old nightmare, but this time it was different, again I was running through the desert responding to my Mother's cry, I got to the tent were she was... this time I could hear my heart beating because of all the fear inside of me, I knew what is happening next... I went in... I see my Mother crying beside somebody, without seeing who it was I knew it was me, the same putrid and disfigured old me... all of the sudden this Lady came in, young lady radiant and beautiful like the sun, I think I have seen her before... I saw her the other day with the entourage accompanying Jesus at the entrance of Jerusalem, only that she was older then, she came in and told my Mother...

- Lady: "Please don't cry... God's Mercy is Great and your son would not be lost, you'll see it if you clean him with the water used to clean Her Son..."

My Mother stopped crying and accepted her offer to use the water for me, as she starts to pour the water I'm not longer the spectator, I was who was being washed! All the putrid skin started to peel away and my skin was as clean as always, all the pus, dead skin, foul smell, ulcers I've got completely healed.

- Helen: "Please, I must know your name."

- Lady: "My name is Mary and this is my family, the sleepy head there is my husband Joseph and the baby in his arms is our son Jesus."

- Helen: "Thank you God almighty, thank you I AM for this miracle, my son is healed!"

The dream change right there, the whole family of Mary disappeared and the whole scene changed, I was in the house were we use to live in Egypt and she saw me with a smile and with her lovely voice told me:

-Helen: "That lady's name was Mary, her husband Joseph and baby Jesus...if you ever encounter them, please my sweet Dismas ...my sweet, sweet, boy Dismas ...serve them in any way you can, because I think God favors them a lot, and if you serve them God will smile on to you".

I woke up with the feeling of a sweet tender kiss from my Mother, I knew that this was I AM talking to me... he was pleased with my prayer... He wants me for Him, He wants me to follow Jesus and serve Him in any way I can! I shouted:

- Dismas: "Thank you I AM!!!, I will follow Jesus!!! Thank you!!!"

I was running as fast as I can, it was already night and truly I have never seen the stars shining that bright... I got into Gestas house.

- Dismas: "Gestas, Gestas, I have to tell you, I have to tell..."

- Jairo: "Hello Dismas."

I was in shock seeing Gestas all covered in blood on the ground and a few guards with Jairo...

- Jairo: "Don't worry, he isn't dead Dismas... the death part will come slowly for both of you, you've been a headache for me Dismas; I have spent a fortune just trying to get you, but in the end everything works out for the good."

- Dismas: "Jairo is not what you think, I have change... I mean I'm sorry about..."

- Jairo: "My Father?, don't feel bad my dear cousin, I know that it was this idiot that kill my father and not you, your friend told everything to a prostitute and she wanted the bounty on your head, actually if you ask me Gestas did me a favor by making me rich, I have control of everything my father had and nobody is going to tell me anymore what to do!!!...but I will never forget the beat down you gave me and because I have been trying very hard to get you, sources have been telling me a lot about you and your past cousin, my revenge will be as sweet as honey."

- Dismas: "Please Jairo, I was mourning and you didn't had respect for my parents, but I'm not the same anymore cousin I've change, all thanks to Jesus the prophet... please I'm sorry about everything."

- Jairo: "The Nazarene? Ha,ha,ha,ha please you are as crazy as all the Jews following him, some of them think he is the Messiah...The Messiah, Ha,ha,ha,ha the Messiah from Nazareth, Ha,ha,ha,ha.... Nothing good has ever come out of Nazareth and the Torah says that the Messiah comes from Bethlehem."

- Dismas: "The Messiah, he's the Messiah?"

- Jairo: "You didn't hear what I just said...?"

- Dismas: "(Crying) He's the Messiah!!"

- Jairo: "Enough you idiot!... soon I will see you suffer beyond your most horrific dreams, it'll be sweet."

- Dismas: "Please, Jairo forgive me... I know that in my heart I have already forgiven you for what you said to my Mother, please forgive me and forgive Gestas for all the harm done cousin."

Then he came and punches me in the face, his friends who were seating in a corner they came and started to hurt me, but the revelation that Jesus may be the Messiah sparkle within my soul like lightning and gave me great hope. After they stopped hitting me the guards took me to jail with Gestas, It was the beginning of Passover and I had to spend it in Jail, for the second time in my life being the first time at Yeshua's... I'm hurting inside and most of it was because of the possibility of Jesus being the Messiah and me not being wherever He was.

I was alone in a cell; Gestas was taken to another cell, I was praying for two days for God to forgive me and if it pleases Him I wanted to seek Jesus and follow Him, it was pretty hard for me these couple of days but I'm praying for a Miracle, I want to follow Jesus wherever He goes.

- "Wake up you piece of dirt!... it's time for your trial, come on."

- Dismas: "Trial?"

The guard took me in front of some priests in which I could see a familiar face, Yeshua... Yeshua was a priest and he was the son of the High priest Caifas which was also present in the room, it was weird because all I did was beat my cousins and his friends, I didn't know why I was in front of them.

- Yeshua: "You don't listen I presume, I told you I never wanted to see you again."

- Dismas: "Peace be with you Yeshua."

- Yeshua: "What? It seems that he wants to teach us how to be decent...Ha,ha,ha,ha, THIS IS THE MAN THAT PRETENDED TO COURT MY DAUGHTER!! HA,HA,HA (Everybody was laughing), THE GRANDAUGHTER OF THE HIGH PRIEST CAIFAS!!! HA,HA,HA (Even more profound laughter).

- Dismas: "Please, I don't know what bad crime besides being in a fight and there's plenty of evidence that is the only thing I did, but do as you want... the peace I have it's enough that I forgive you beforehand."

- Yeshua: "Well it seems that you have grown up since our last conversation... but before this is over you need to know that whatever is that you have will be crushed because of the charges against you, the thing is... I wasn't the one collecting all this information, neither was this holy tribunal... but it was all the people that had something against you... you friend Gestas was found guilty and was given to the romans to be crucified soon."

- Dismas: "...."

They had Jairo telling everything how it happened during the years between us and how it ended with the death of his father.

- Jairo: "We all know Gestas was the one that killed my father, we know that this two were partners and everybody in Bethlehem knew that father and Dismas had a problem, all of the sudden his partner in crime appears in the right place at the right time and kills him!!... What a coincidence!!"

- Yeshua: "What do you have to say about that, Dismas?"

- Dismas: "It's true that we didn't see eye to eye, but I didn't want his death, is true that Gestas is my friend... unfortunately he knew that I had problems with him because I beat his son and his two friends with my own fists, but I'm not a killer."

- Jairo: "Really?... All of you of this respected and honorable tribunal need to know that I have credible information that Dismas was the person involved in the assassination of a Jew named John more than a decade ago..."

- Dismas: "What?... stop this Jairo that's a lie!... stop all of this, this is just not true gentleman, I want to see this proof, it's just not true!"

(A lot of murmuring among the people and priests at the tribunal).

- Yeshua: "All quiet, please quiet...what proof you have on this."

- Jairo: "Back then Dismas was a thief coming from Egypt that had to retire because of a promise made to his mother this we know from Gestas, but in my tracking of Dismas everywhere where I had spies, I came with a young men that use to work for Mr. John at the tavern where Dismas used to work; this person use to help Mr. John preparing meals at the tavern while Dismas ran the tables. The day that Mr. John was found dead in his own tavern, a man called Isaac was purchasing some things for Mr. John at the Market, he came back and found his boss dead on the ground."

- Dismas: "That can't be, I left him breathing and alive, it can't be!."

- Isaac: "That's true members of this honorable tribunal."

- Yeshua: "Please, who are you?"

-Isaac: "I'm the son of Mishra and Daniel a farmer from Judea, that day I'll never forget... all that Mr. Jairo spoke is the truth, I was running late to the tavern I got delayed because of a puppet show in the market, I noticed that I was late and since Mr. John was a very impatience boss I ran, when I was near the tavern when I saw Dismas running away from it, once I got inside I saw Mr. John on the ground beat down and covered in his own blood... he had his face all swollen, his last words were... Dismas."

- Isaac: " I went to the romans but when I got there, all the romans there were drunk and when I finally got to speak to someone, they punch me and put me in jail because they thought that I was there admitting that I killed somebody, a week later after they listened to me I got out... Nobody did anything because those days there were riots all over the city, I went to the tribunal and they took notice of it then I went back to Judea."

- Yeshua: "How Mr. Jairo got in touch with you Mr. Isaac?"

- Isaac: "I got the news through a friend that a reward was given for information to get Dismas from Egypt, the only guy I knew from Egypt was the Dismas whom I used to work with, so it had to be him... when I got in contact with Jairo, he gave me a description of the person involved and It turned out to be the same old Dismas that used to work for Mr. John, the thing is that I didn't know where he went, everybody thought that he was again living in Egypt, not Bethlehem."

I broke down in tears... I just couldn't believe that Mr. John was dead!... this has to be some sort of a joke, some sick joke.

- Jairo: (Whispering in his ear) now where is that semblance of yours? Where is that light in your face?, all I see is anguish and despair... I told you boy... as sweet as honey."

- Dismas: "YOU LIE, YOU ALL LIED!!!... Mr. John can't be dead... I left him breathing...!"

- Yeshua: "So it is confirmed... you beat him to death."

- Dismas: "I... I... left him breathing (profoundly crying)."

- Jairo: "Now there, how can you tell how a 50 year old man was sick and then you crushed him with you slick fists and lead him to his death."

- Dismas: "Oh God, I AM... I'm so sorry!... please forgive me!!! I didn't know, I didn't want that to happen!"

- Yeshua: "It is such an easy verdict, do we all agreed?"

I didn't hear anything anymore after that; I kept going in my mind that day over and over again... I didn't know he was sick... maybe this is a bad dream, a horrible dream... then I saw Yeshua standing up with all the other Jews.

- Yeshua: "It is written in the law... you took a life so your life shall be taken from you, you will be given to Romans for crucifixion, take him away!"

The life of me wanted to flee my very flesh, I couldn't believe it... I was a murderer. I was taken to a cell down from where I was, we spend the night there me and Gestas, poor guy... he was out of it; next day came I didn't sleep at all, not one bit... we were taken out to the Romans who were expecting us, then Jairo was there and shouted from a distance:

- Jairo: "As sweet as honey."

He turned away as I was taken by the guards, I loudly replied:

- Dismas: "I'm sorry Jairo for your father... I forgiv..."

- Smack!!

A Roman soldier just hit me in my side with the back of a spear, all the air of my lungs came out... I couldn't say what I wanted to say, I was surrounded with the soldier's laughter but in my mind I kept repeating: "I FORGIVE YOU." It was Passover, we were told any day now we were going to get crucified, so I started to pray more and more like never in my life, inside my cell there was this guy also waiting to be crucified, his name was Barabbas.

- Barabbas: "That is not necessary my friend, there is no God... only ourselves, only ourselves putted us in this mess and nobody is going to get us out of it."

- Dismas: "How can you say that, you have no fear of what is beyond this life? Who but God put those stars out there? You need to say your prayers my friend, because we all need God's Mercy."

- Barabbas: "Mercy...? What's Mercy...? That somebody could be there and tell you everything is alright? Mercy is going to make you feel good for yourself when your fill of bad deeds, can Mercy take you bad deeds away... forever?

- Dismas: "Mercy is God and God created us, if you are created is because something good happened in order for you to exist, look at the sun and the stars... there's nothing out there more beautiful than that, the moon is gorgeous, so when we look up and marvel about those things the one that created us sees us and I presume that He marvels too when we are good like He is, if we behave badly it is written that we are never going to see Him, I want His Mercy so much now at the end of my life, so I could be able to see Him with no shame, so now I repent of my sins and I'm expecting His Mercy, that is my most sincere hope...that is the base of my prayer."

- Barabbas: "Ha, ha, ha, ha... how stupid you are my friend... God doesn't exist... what It exists is the love of the people, the love of the PEOPLE!... when you are a winner everybody is your friend, I change that for God any day; I mean, where is He when we need Him...Israel the chosen nation amongst all nations and we are slaves to the Romans, when I got arrested I just knew there was no God... HA, HA, HA, HA, HA."

- Dismas: "I will pray for you so you might understand sooner rather than later my friend."

- Barabbas: "Sure, do what you think is good for you; I just know that I have no salvation... Where is God when my crucifixion begins? When me and the men that fought the Romans were trying to do something good for Israel?, unfortunately my friends were the only ones that wanted to fight the romans so bad, we wanted the whole town to back us up, but the people in this town are all cowards... COWARDS!"

- Dismas: "Uprising?"

- Barabbas: "Yes, we fought the romans... a small group of brave men, we needed the whole town to fight with us, but we got nothing instead; we didn't do much to the Romans, it started when we killed a tax collector that was harassing our people with the taxes, he was accompanied by a couple of guards... We killed the tax collector, correction... as I killed him! But the guards then called other guards, and this is how the uprising began."

- Dismas: "No remorse?"

- Barabbas: "No... This tax collector was an ally to the romans, any time you can kill people like that... is a good day. We try to get the people involved and we had some swords hidden... we started as five then quickly we had forty men, we knew that the romans would try to get us and the fight came forth, but didn't last long... I was the only one that remained out of forty brave men, we were massacred... we failed to involve more people, why?...because they're cowards, COWARDS!

As I felt more and more near to my death, I prayed harder and harder... I included my friend Gestas and Barabbas in my prayers, anytime now they are coming to get us... to be crucified. Crucifixion, it was the ultimate insult... nobody wanted to get crucified not only because of the obvious, dying... but it was how, it was the most profound lack of respect for any human being, everybody feared the crucifixion, it was such an insult that people use to mock who got the cross...

I never saw anybody being crucified but as I was told by Barabbas, they would nail us there and leave us to rot as an example to whoever wanted to defy authority, it was the ultimate humiliation.

- Laughter –

- Dismas: "What is going on? Are they coming to get us?"

- Barabbas: "No... Look a man is getting scourged!"

- Dismas: "Who... what?"

I couldn't believe my eyes it was... Jesus! Jesus was getting scourged! What is going on? He is the Messiah! I don't understand! I mean as I look on his naked back His flesh is being torn apart, please no!!! noooo!!! I was crying... I didn't have strength in my voice and my tears ran like a river; all I did was cry in despair.

- Dismas: "Please I AM, God Almighty...please assist Jesus with your unrelentless Love, please hear me God, I know I don't deserve any of Your attention but this man is a good man, give Him Your assistance."

They stopped beating Him up with the whip to star punching Him straight in the face, saying "who hit you" as they laughed in their sick game, mocking Him by doing a King's reverence, one of the Romans made something out of a tree and put it in His Head and everybody was shouting "Hail to the King of the Jews!"

It was unbearable to watch, a Roman captain got angry at them because they were instructed only to scourge Him, they took him away and all just kept laughing like it was some sort of a game for them. I was in a corner crying for hours; with a feeling of a big nothing ... The only thing I kept hearing in my mind was "As sweet as Honey." I was being thrown into a big nothing; I can't stay like this...

I have my hopes in I AM my Savior, I Hope that Jesus is too… and another thing came into my mind: "Mary, Joseph and Jesus if you ever encounter them, serve them in any way you can my sweet Dismas, they are favored by God." I started saying: "Mother… Mother, tell I AM that I loved Him, but I failed to serve Them!."

Several Hours later I thought they were coming for us, but they only came for Barabbas.

- Barabbas: "See boy what did I tell you… God doesn't exist."

- Dismas: "I'll pray for you Barabbas, so you could see the Sweet Mercy of God."

They only took him and I don't know why.

- Dismas: "I AM hear me please, hear the prayer of a soon to be dead man… have Mercy on us, have Mercy on Barabbas so that he may see Your awesome Power, for Gestas so that You reveal on to him your Love, give us the strength to forgive and forget, give us the strength to repent with a sincere heart, so that we could see Your Love without the shame of our bad deeds."

Then they came for me finally, kicking me around a bit to force me out… they tied the Cross on to me, I'm seeing Gestas fighting back but the poor guy is no match for them, they punch him in the groin with the back of a spear, he was cursing them all saying: "Beasts, beasts, my behind is more clean than you! Beasts…!" when I started to walk with this Cross, I saw Jesus in the back… oh! Sweet I AM, Jesus is all swollen, He's completely disfigured by all the violence He has suffered, it wasn't a pretty sight… they placed that big cross on to Him, Jesus couldn't breathe well and they place the cross on top of Him without a rope like me…

As we walked towards the hill, some people were crying for Jesus, others were spiting in our faces, others throwing things at us; that crowd is more in number and more hostile than the crowd crying for Jesus, then I saw a familiar face, Barabbas…

He was in the crowd, a free man! I was shocked to know that God made a miracle with him, the miracle of a second chance! As I walked passed him, he saw me... I saw him... I just smiled, he seemed to be in disbelieve that he was out and we were in... I continue my journey on to the Golgotha... then I heard Jesus.

- Jesus: "Daughters of Jerusalem do not weep for me; weep for yourselves and for your children. For the time will come when you will say, 'Blessed are the barren women, the wombs that never bore and the breasts that never nursed!' Then "'they will say to the mountains, "Fall on us!" and to the hills, "Cover us!"' For if men do these things when the tree is green, what will happen when it is dry?"

The green wood, when wood is dry no fruit can be expected from it, they are taking down the green one... one that could give much fruit to them and they were doing this knowingly, after some distance Jesus fell again with His cross, the romans pushed us further along so we proceed without Jesus, we walked towards the hill without Him.

- Dismas: "I AM give me the strength to recognize your doing, give me the strength to recognize Your Mercy"

We went to the top and they took my clothes violently; thank God I had something to cover my genitals!... I was seeing how Gestas was calling the Romans names as he was being nailed, it was horrendous; they put me down with the cross... it was my turn, fear kicked in and I was trying to get my arms out of the ropes... the first nail went in.

- Dismas: "AAAHHHAH.....HHHH, BEASTSSSS... BEASTSS."

The second nail to my left hand went in, when they were preparing to put the ones in my feet Jesus arrived... I was trying not to curse them but it wasn't easy, the third nail went in at my feet and it was even more painful, Gestas was already up, they were trying to put me up when Jesus got nailed, the prophet didn't curse anybody, he didn't say nothing to the Romans...

Nothing at all!, He suffered the same pain as us with the nails, but he never even gave anybody a bad look... they put Him up with us, then looking up into the Heavens I heard Him say:

- Jesus: "Father, forgive them, for they do not know what they are doing."

He was calling God Father? Jesus the prophet was His Son?... All doubts came crumbling down like the walls of Jericho after the trumpets sounded, He was truly the Messiah! Thank You I AM, thank You!... for letting me recognize Your Mercy right there in my face in your son Jesus. The Romans started to play for Jesus clothes like it was some type of trophy, as the people began to be nastier with Jesus, but He never turned away His face from them.

- "He saved others; let him save himself if he is the Christ of God, the Chosen One." (Others they just said "Yes, save yourself").

The Romans were mocking Him.

-"Save yourself if you're the King of the Jews."

Gestas was pretty much out of himself saying the same thing as the Romans and the people:

- Gestas: "Aren't you the Christ? Save yourself and us!"

- Dismas: "Don't you fear God, since you are under the same sentence? We are punished justly, for we are getting what our deeds deserve. But this man has done nothing wrong... Jesus, remember me when you come into your kingdom."

- Jesus: "Amen, amen I say to you, today you will be with me in paradise."

I felt at Peace finally! I AM was smiling at me through Jesus... what an awesome God you are I AM; the Mother of Jesus was there and witnessed all, she was the same person I saw in my dreams, she had her eyes swollen because of all the tears she cried over Her Son, the man next to Her was in some sort of disbelieve, like this wasn't happening.

- Jesus: "Dear woman, here is your son"

- Jesus: (To the person next to His Mother) "Here is your mother."

It was late when everything became dark; the sun stopped shinning, when Jesus said:

- Jesus: "Eloí, Eloí, lammá sabactani"

 My God, my God, why have you forsaken me, He said? Minutes later with a loud voice Jesus gave His Spirit to I AM; it was all dark for hours... immediately after He died an earthquake started shaking the hill! I don't know how did our crosses didn't fell down, it was a big one for sure and pretty scary thing, a lot of people were running like sheep with a wolf behind their tails...

Gestas was still alive and started laughing hard like a madman, poor Gestas he wasn't himself, as for me? My pain wasn't pain anymore, I had my heart filled with joy as I was seeing the end of my life... finally, I was content.

It was getting harder and harder to breathe; the people that ran for cover from the earthquake slowly came back, most of them pounding their fists on to their chests, some ripping their clothes and putting dust into their heads as a sign of mourning, Gestas wouldn't stop laughing...

- Dismas: "The sky is bluer than ever Mother! I hope that you are pleased with the son you raised, in the end I found my way... I love you Helen, I love you I AM, I love you Jesus."

- (CRUSH!).

- Dismas: "AAAAAGGHHHHH!!!!"

- Gestas: "AAAAAGGHHHHH!!!!"

They came and hit my legs with something; oh my God I could see the bone out my legs! Gestas was in the same situation, they crush his legs to... Oh Sweet God have Mercy on us, they went to Jesus but He was already dead! Oh this pain is horrible!! Then the soldier used a spear to Jesus chest and incredibly blood and water burst down, some were marveled as the soldier that thrust the spear to His chest was in shock and two romans had to pull him away...

Oh! Lord Gestas is dead!! Oh God come and take me now, I beg you I AM! I was hanging from my arms, they pain was tremendous, I started to fell asleep and I saw for the last time the face of Jesus Mother Mary swollen with tears... Jesus you had your Mother to cry over you and many friends, I didn't had nobody after my Mother Helen, please receive me in your kingdom, I AM let this be, let thhhiiis...sss b.bb..eee (sigh)....

I opened my eyes... How curious, no pain...started to look around and I saw my body for the last time hanging from the cross, involuntarily I started to go down to a dark place were a lot of people were, crying and lamenting all this voices at once scaring me more and more, funny that even though it was dark you had a sense of how many people were there... millions! I started to descend and I have to say that I was scared beyond words, suddenly light was coming my way, beautiful light as the voices change from cry and lamenting to voices pleading and begging to be released. This Light was getting brighter and brighter, wait! It's Jesus! Yes, Jesus glowing like the sun with many souls behind Him as all the other souls He passed by were pleading their case to Him, He came straight to me and said... "Let's go Dismas."

We started to ascend above that place as people that stayed behind began to lament and cry even harder, we did fly through the earth into the sky and above, it was beyond our dreams... as we ascended we saw Angels singing and praising the ONE WHO GAVE HIMSELF AS SACRIFICE, never heard something more beautiful, as somebody touch me from behind...

- Dismas: "Mother... Father!"

They smiled to me they weren't old anymore... Hey I wasn't 35 years old anymore! I felt like 20, we were in such a happiness kind of shock, we were seeing the heavens as we fly with the Jesus, we got to a place where everything was like our home, but more awesome! I mean the thickest grass I have ever seen, angels everywhere and a river so clear that you could see the bottom from the shore, light everywhere! It was like we were living in the arms of the sun... it was amazing.

- Helen: "Dismas ...you did well, I am happy for you and us my sweet boy."

- Simon: "Yes Dismas, I am happy that I was your father... in the end is not what you use to do that define your destiny, you destiny is define in an eternal proportion once you recognize that God loves you and you don't want to offend Him, all you want to do is, please Him... I'm so happy for you and for us."

- Dismas: "Thank you I AM for your Mercy through Jesus...your Son."

-Jesus: "Are you talking about me?"

We all laughed...

- Jesus: "You see all this Dismas? Everything is for all of you who believed in my Father's Mercy, He has His Glorious Love for all Men that believes in Me, from now until the end of times... all men in order to come to My Father's Kingdom has to come through Me, your luck finally changed Dismas... for the better."

- Dismas: "(I kneeled before Him) Thank you my King, I want to do what I've should have done back home and follow you to your Father I AM."

- Jesus: "Once I present you to Him He will be pleased, I know He is because you never doubted even in your darkest hour, my Father granted your prayer by showing to you Mercy itself, you recognized who I was, repented and Mercy was given opening the doors of paradise for you."

- Dismas: "Thank you."

- Jesus: "I have to go now; my disciples need me... stay here until I come back so I could present you all to my Father Almighty."

We all kneel down and said a loud Yes unto the King, and then He disappeared... Angels were everywhere, I saw Adam and Eve, Samson, King Saul's son Johnathan were among the crowd that came from the prison we left behind, some with great merits and some others without merits like me, It was awesome, you could feel waves of love everywhere, the most curious thing it was the flowers...they were singing!: "Glory to God Almighty for Jesus the King of Kings".

You could know in an instant the life of those people there with you, what they did, their moments of joy, there greatest accomplishments, their families... it was a great feeling, I could talk with my lips or not because I could talk through my thoughts, it was AWESOME.

Then something Great was about to happen, all the angels, us, everybody there put their attention to Jerusalem... Jesus was resurrecting! His whole Holy body, broken and disfigured as I remembered there on the Cross, was glowing like the sun, clean and glorious...

Angels everywhere started to praised Him and sing in Honor of Him, we also heard from the depths of the abyss the devil shouting like the beast he is over his defeat, he couldn't do anything it was the will of God and His will is within Jesus, all Glory to Him!

Jesus stood up Glorious and Beautiful from the crypt, an angel rolled the stone and the Romans ran in fright, everything that the King did...we saw.

Also other things unfolding around His Beautiful Name, we saw when those Romans were paid for their silence and said to all that the disciples took Jesus, we saw when Thomas said to the disciples he needed to put his hand into His side and touch with his fingers Jesus wounds, we saw how the King disguise Himself in front of Mary Magdalene, when He appeared to Peter, when He appeared to the two disciples in Emmaus, when He appeared to disciples with close doors, when eight days passed and Jesus appeared to Thomas, when He appeared to the disciples in the Sea of Galilee... it was all marvelous.

The day had come to receive the King with all the Honor and Glory, and that's if you would like to call it a day because here in heaven there is no nights or days, they explained to me that it was called eternity... All angels received the King with praises, we kneeled to the Holy Son of I AM as He entered the palace, throughout all Heaven they sang "Glory to the King of Kings, the Lamb of God, the Son of God, the only one worthy of recognition and praise in unity to God and the Holy Spirit", they repeated this song over and over again as He entered in the palace where I AM was, once He was inside we heard a voice like a thousand thunders: "IT IS DONE"... within our souls we knew that phrase was said from Almighty God, saying that men were freed at last from the bondage of sin and death didn't had power anymore, we were all rejoicing because Jesus took His seat beside I AM.

Immediately we crossed the river to see Him in order to be judged, when my turn came... a sea of love overflowed as I entered, a sea of love welcoming me to the Holy Tribunal a huge tornado of tenderness upon my soul, with each word The King said to me it was like He was hugging me!

- Jesus: "Dismas... you were a man that took the wrong path during your life, you were a thief, a criminal, a murderer, although you didn't know until the very end that you were, violence and anger took the best of you and evil you became, fortunately for you... you've got the Treasure of all the Heavens my sweet thief, you've got My Mercy which from now and forever this Treasure is for all who comes to get crucified with me, many will enjoy the endless sea of Love from My Father and I, you suffered with Me and came to Me for redemption... from now and forever all will remember you as Saint Dismas, your repentance was as beautiful as your Greek name for sunset...from now on pray to my Beautiful Father for all Thieves, criminals and all mankind to convert."

Jesus raised His right Hand on to me and without words He said to my soul: "Welcome child... welcome home." As all angels started to sing Hallelujah praised the Lamb of God, I walked towards my eternity with a smile... the saint's houses were being built for all the future Saints to worship The Father and Jesus... but His Love didn't stopped there, The Power of Love of the Heavens burst from the palace like a million suns into one we understood that it was The Holy Spirit of God moving towards earth, going there to be with the disciples and all who gets baptized and accepts Jesus as Lord... We all Kneeled before the Mighty Strength of the Holy Spirit, we saw how the Holy Spirit embrace each of the disciple's hearts giving them Great Love.

I'm still amazed by His Mercy... me, a thief in heaven? Wake up Dismas!!! This is the greatest dream ever! Better yet don't wake up, I was looking down to earth and I'm seeing the disciples working in favor of the Kingdom, I'm seeing Peter which betrayed Jesus, Thomas Who didn't believe, Paul was populating with Martyrs the heavens at the time, all this knowledge given to us by His Mighty Power! He has shown Great Mercy to me a thief... the kingdom of God is full of that: thieves, prostitutes, traitors, deceivers and the list goes on and on, all who repented in time and recognized something that was far Greater than life itself, we recognized His Love performing and embrace it as we all repented from our bad deeds, we placed our trust in Jesus, who is My King and Savior... and I pray that you find Him and get the Treasure of the Heavens today like I did, the Treasure... His Sweet Mercy. Amen.

My Sweet Jesus

With a smile I accept your Love...
with open arms I accept your Kingdom...
with joy, You accept my repentance...
My Lord, My Sweet Jesus.

My sins are erased...
My path You create...
with joy I embrace...
My Lord, My Sweet Jesus.

My flesh I need to deny...
The world now I must fight...
But the only way I could win...
Is with my Lord, My Sweet Jesus.

I child I must be...
In your arms I will dream...
As we walk to the death hill...
It's alright I have my Lord, My Sweet Jesus.

Book II:

THE ART OF WAR.

PREFACE

It was a good day like any other day for the bullies; the Roman Empire was providing service for their client, Herod the great died and his kingdom divided in three portions, in which one later wasn't actually a kingdom, but only a Roman section as Archaelus son of Herod, was given only power amongst the people of Judea, it was a turbulent times as many uprisings were crushed and many people were killed. Longinus was a good soldier militarily speaking, obedient, skillful, well liked among his peers, and loved by his superiors, it was a time were being away from home too long could change a beast into a monster, the prayer of an innocent man and a miracle that gained back his eyesight, changed him forever. That allegiance to the armies of Rome after that miracle would change to desertion, those days to desert the army was to find a death warrant.

PROLOGUE

Captain instructed us not kill him as he wanted a prisoner for Pontius Pilate, this Barabbas came to us with his toy sword and I was seeing him with my one good eye coming towards me fast, in my mind I recreated how I was going to deal with him... I was going to cut short the distance between me and him by leaping towards him with my shield, so I took a big step towards him as my Captain was yelling: "Don't kill him Longinus!!", and of course it was the right move by me, I mean... everything I thought in my mind right there in battle, it always work, this is one of many things that make me the best soldier among my peers; I took all the air out from this Jew as I smash him a little bit with my shield, I kicked his little sword out and we took him captive... it was a good day. Nothing is better for a soldier than a little bit of action, now as we walk back to the praetorian, I just know we'll have some fun with this prisoner, hopefully somebody comes by soon, so this criminal doesn't get crucified alone.

I'm a soldier of Rome! I'm a soldier of Rome and crying is only for the enemy!...ha, ha, ha, ha, this guy Barabbas was crying like a girl when we got him, I'm a good soldier of Rome and I've seen everything, I used to cry in my first month of service, I got beaten by my peers multiple of times because of it, after that I've build some type of an invisible armor around me that forbid me to feel anything, after wars and wars all over the world. I was sent to this forsaken place, yes I'm unable to feel pity, I'm unable to feel mercy, I'm unable to feel love... After my first war and the killings of hundreds of men, penetrating woman wasn't any good for me, though I've had hundreds of them under my belt, participating with my troops in this pleasures: taking slaves, gold, goods, happened in every war... it wasn't only the blood I've spilled, but the hundreds of men that I've butchered and my fellow brothers in arms I've seen dead in a gruesome way, all of that and more made me who I am today.

We were called to squash an uprising here in Jerusalem, a tax collector was killed... I don't know why we are going after this assassination if the man was a Jew, but word of the mouth was that this tax collector was friends with Pontius Pilate, when we got to the plaza we found the body of this Jew and Captain notice that the man was a roman citizen, then we got our blood flowing and burning in flames as we charged this cowards... it was a massacre, they were trying to get the people involved, but most were fleeing; the first Jew I got I just smash His neck with the edge of my shield, it was boring to fight in formation but the Captain was big believer in us following protocol and within protocol we've always succeeded, I mean less dead Romans! Anyways, after cracking wide open some heads, the only one left was this guy crying out loud cowards! Cowards! COWARDS!!!

We were all laughing at him...

The days passed by and the troop was still anxious about that exchange of blood, and we had a potential uprising again as we were given the orders to scourged this guy name Jesus, they told us that He names himself as the "King of the Jews", Josephus and Lacius scourged Him with 40 lashes and unfortunately for this Jesus, Josephus and Lacius were the most strongest guys in the troop, they had a feast with his flesh; we retuned him to Pilate, as they weren't too happy because he was pretty beat up... we were all laughing.

- Josephus: "I'm getting tired of all this Jews."

- Lacius: "We are all tired my friend."

- Longinus: "Well we've got work to do; I think a little later we are going to crucify Barabbas and two other guys..."

What do you know... we had a crucifixion alright, but it was Jesus the King of the Jews... we laughed hard, because we heard that one of His crimes was that He called Himself the Son of God, well... we did what we had to do in the Golgotha, I was mad that Barabbas were let go by Pilate, as the crucifixion happened, Jesus was praying to God for all of us, that shook me a bit... my laughter disappeared by the Man's prayer:

- Jesus: "Father forgive them they do not know what they do!"

Later one of the thieves was pleading to Jesus to forgive Him and when He (Jesus), entered His Kingdom, please do remember him.

- Jesus: "Amen, Amen I say to you will be with me in paradise!"

Jesus was forgiving a thief of his deeds, that surprise me a lot because there's nothing more distasteful than a thief... they have no respect for anybody. Anyways the display of power was the one that caught my attention, the sun erased from the sky as an earthquake shook the entire earth, at that time I thought that we... I have done the biggest mistake of my life.

We killed the Son of God! We killed the Son of God alright... this was our mistake, one of many... First, the order to scourge Him was given and we were good at scourging people... every whip given was with the force of a horse, each whip that He suffered gave way to His live flesh, we were all laughing because we heard that He called Himself "The King of the Jews"... King of what we hated... Jews; some of us stayed in this forsaken land for too long as we provided military service to the Roman Empire, the service used to be 16 years, but Tiberius Cesar prolonged the service by 20 years; we were all laughing as we finish Him, Lacius made a crown out of some tree for the King, a crown of thorns we put in His head as we all shouted:

- "Hail King of the Jews."

The Jew went out to Pilate but came back right after we send a criminal called Barabbas there, He came back to be crucify... we were confused for a little while because it was rare to have someone scourged and right after crucified, but we went ahead and follow our orders like the good soldiers we were, Jesus was His name... a man in suffering due to the good job we did, He was all swollen because we kept striking Him in the head, it wasn't a pretty sight to see, but I didn't gave it much thought, we prepare Him and two others scheduled for crucifixion. At the Golgotha with all three crucified, we started to play for the clothes of the King, I don't remember if Josephus or Lacius won those clothes... anyways what I remember is that Jesus didn't returned a word to whom tried to humiliate Him, not even a bad look.

- Jesus: "Elí, Elí, lamá sabactani."

- Jesus: "I thirst."

I didn't know what that meant, one of the soldiers by the name of Stephaton took a sponge soak in with vinegar, then he place it into his mouth... Jesus took it freely... then He looked up and said:

- Jesus: "It is finished."

- Jesus: (Loudly)"Father, into your hands I commend my spirit."

My captain said: "The man was innocent beyond doubt." Since before the third hour the skies gradually became darker and darker, suddenly after Jesus died a big earthquake began and everybody started to run in distress... I shouted:

- "Truly, this was the Son of God!"

I was so afraid that God Himself would've come out the heavens to kill us, after an eternity, the earthquake stopped and some light came to us... it was a strange situation, some Jews came and ask our captain to hurry up on the crucifixions because the Sabbath was coming.

- Captain: "Longinus! Finish this now..."

- Longinus: "Yes captain."

With a bone crusher I crippled one of the two men were along Jesus as Lacius did the other criminal, I knew he was dead... so I didn't even bother to look, but my captain signal to Jesus.

- Longinus: "He's dead Captain."

- Captain: "Make sure."

I took my spear and thrust my lance into his side, immediately blood and water flowed out... my hands and my face was covered with blood and water, I kneeled down looking to the crucified, I've never felt so much Love in my entire life!!! Everything was so clear to me now and I was running blind in my left eye, it was a miracle! I could see clearly now... Jesus was the Son of God, the Son of God and we Killed Him! I was fighting within me, struggling with guilt building up in me, at the same time enjoying true Love for the very first time, the overwhelming feeling of Love was greater than the guilt, I knew I was pardoned for what I did, His blood and water make me realize about something that Jesus said earlier, something that I took for granted.

- Jesus: "Father forgive them, they do not know what they do."

Some of my colleagues had to take me away while on my knees, I wasn't hearing what my captain was saying to me, I was in shock with all this love pouring down; I'm a soldier and I've seen wars, I've killed men, I've seen thousands of crucifixions, but this one is the one that made me feel again... FEEL! This is how I was able to fight all this wars and uprisings, not feeling were something that the army taught me in order to do my job, Jesus caught my soul and with his Love and this is my declaration.

My name is Longinus born and raised in the Roman Empire, I served two Caesars Augustus and now Tiberius, I've been in the military for 14 years and this is my declaration, the declaration of the freedom I've got through Jesus.

I've been in many wars, I've seen many horrors, I've done terrible things in the name of Caesar, after so many years in service I thought that I've seen it all, but nothing prepared me for this... We carried out our orders, we laughed and played with the victim to the point that He no longer had a face, we disfigured Him, He was all swollen and when we nailed Him to the cross He prayed for us, I regained my eye sight by the gush of blood and water that came from His side as I struck my lance in...

- Longinus: "Stop, stop I say!... I'm alright now, I'm alright..."

- Lascius: "Are you sure my friend? The Captain was calling your name and you didn't answer..."

- Longinus: "Yes I'm fine..."

I took my spear, went to the Captain and apologized for not hearing what he was saying...

- Captain: "What happened there Longinus?"

- Longinus: "Sorry my Captain, some of the blood poured in my face and now my left eye has regained sight."

- Captain: "You're joking right? We all noticed your limitations on your left flank and thought that you were becoming blind, but now you say that you have recovered from it?... By the blood?"

- Longinus: "Yes my Captain, you know I would never lie to you..."

After that exchange he said to me with a gesture to remain quiet, then a Jew came forth with an order from Pontius Pilate himself about releasing the body of Jesus to him, the Captain gave us the order to unnail Jesus and give it to the Jew and His family; Lacius was given the job to release Jesus at the top of the cross, Lascius tied Jesus with a long veil provided by Jesus family as he took the nails out, then slowly he brought down God's Son... Poor woman, the Mother of Jesus had her eyes all swollen and rivers of tears, some other women were loudly crying, She was crying in silent profusely. Captain also gave us the order to help them by transporting the body to its final destination... Lacius, Josephus and I were preparing to go there with the dead body of Jesus.

- Captain: "Longinus!, only two are needed...let Josephus and Lacius go and come with me."

I couldn't refuse an order of my Captain, we went to the city afterwards... on the way we saw some people marveled because of some people that were dead came back to life, most of the troop didn't believe that, but I knew that it was all about Jesus death and God showing His power; most of the troop were doing the things as we the soldiers of Rome use to do, only Stephaton, Aphrodisius and me were in a shock state, we refuse to talk, we refuse to rise our heads, to be put in this position by our leaders was an awkward one. We got to the praetorian keep and we were allowed to rest for the afternoon, later my Captain called me.

- Captain: "Longinus... we just killed an innocent man, I want you to stay focus because we don't know when this Jews will try to kill us in another fight, I know that this is no ordinary man, I know that you received a gift from this Holy man by recovering your eye sight, please... you're a good soldier, even though you were going blind I'll take you over the whole troop, you're loyal and the best fighter I've got, we need to do our jobs in name of Caesar and mother Rome."

- Longinus: "I thank you my Captain for your words, you're right, we killed a Holy man... I'll try to concentrate Captain on the job at hand, but right now this is too much for me, we have been in many wars together... I was always detached to my feelings and emotions for the sake of the job and mother Rome, today I feel ashamed, I don't know what happened or why this man was there in the first place, why did I mocked Him, why did I punched Him, why did I thrust Him, why did I killed Him..."

-Captain: "You know that we don't question our orders around here, we obey them, unfortunately it has been a common thing to have a little fun with the prisoners, but that is what give us an edge in battle, how do you think we can go about our daily business? This is taught and you know this, being able to detached ourselves from Mercy give us the edge to strike with no hesitation, I know what you are saying Longinus and to tell you the truth I don't like it, but we are soldiers and soldiers follow orders even if they don't like it, if we don't eventually we die... it's them or us and I choose us."

- Longinus: "Captain I know this and you also know that I'm the type of soldier that never questioned anything, but please answer me this... we know this was a Holy man...right?

-Captain: "Indeed He was."

- Longinus: "You don't fear the afterlife knowing that you have killed a Holy man Captain? Because I do now and if it's true that this was the Son of God, there's not going to be an afterlife for any of us!"

- Captain: (Deep sigh) "Ok, what do you want from me Longinus? I have to follow orders, it'll be two more years until my service is up and I could go back home to my wife and kids, I know that you don't have a family my friend, but I'd like to go back to them... regarding about the afterlife, your right but what else could we do? we didn't know until the very end this man was Holy, what can we do?... there's nothing we could do but live our lives and hope for the best."

- Longinus: "Well, at least we could try and get more information about this Jesus, gathering more information is how we could choose what battles to fight..."

- Captain: "Yes, well said Longinus, I have a friend posted in some forsaken city and this friend of mine mentioned Jesus once, I think his coming in a few months, he'll tell us what he knows."

We spoke all through the night about all the things that happened during the crucifixion, how Pilate didn't want to crucify Him, how Jesus own people gave Him to us and painfully... how we beat Him so much; Captain also told me that he ordered me not to go and transport the Holy body, that some Jews were concerned about how Jesus could be stolen by their disciples, since I was a little out of focus in the field, my Captain decided against me going.

Next day I was still sleeping, I asked permission to be off for a few days until I could clear my head a little bit, didn't want to eat, didn't want to be seen and the guilt about His death was growing stronger and stronger, it was a horrible feeling; by midday I was sleeping again and I had a strange dream:

I was at the Golgotha crucifying Him again and again, but He didn't die, He didn't curse at me like the other two crucified were, He was just there suffering a lot, He couldn't die only until I thrust my lance in His side once, He immediately died... The whole earth started to shake vigorously, a lot of dead people rise alive from their tombs and shouted: "The Son of God has died for our sins, hail to the King of Kings", I was down on my knees crying thinking, "what have I done!"

Blood and Water gush from His side coming down like a wave throughout the whole world, reaching inside all men and gave them a new heart. I was amazed with this great Miracle, then the heavens opened and a cloud took Him away to God, the heavens closed and a voice said: "Thank You Father for your Mercy", I didn't understood right away, but the thief that was beside Him appeared before me in a beautiful and radiant white cloak, He said: "You don't understand?... do you remember what He said? Father forgive them, they do not know what they do" and everything was much clearer for me...

I was forgiven, the feeling of Love and forgiveness out the Blood and Water in my face was true, my guilt disappeared in an instant as the thief started to disappeared, I wanted to ask questions but he didn't let me, he was completely gone with this phrase: "Now it's time to persevere in Him, soon will be your time to fight."

I woke up that afternoon experiencing great marvel, and the guilt inside of me it was almost gone, it seems to me that all that participated in the crucifixion were all pardoned! What a nice feeling knowing this, but still had a lot of questions, still with a lot of doubts; later that night found Lacius crying silently in a corner with a money bag.

- Longinus: "What is going on Lacius, what happened?"

- Lacius: "I'm sorry, I'm sorry... (Loudly chanting) I'm a soldier of Rome, I'm a soldier of Rome and crying is only..."

- Longinus: "For the enemy?...come one Lacius is me your talking to, that soldier crap is for the superiors not me... what happened...?"

- Lacius: "We were posted outside were Jesus was buried at the third hour of the next day an earthquake shaken the whole area, an angel came down from the sky, his face gave us much fear as we only saw lightning out of his face, he came down and rolled the stone away from the entrance, we had to fight our frozen legs in order to flee but as he was nearing us we fell like rocks in the ground!"

- Longinus: "What!!!..."

- Lacius: "I woke up first and then woke up Josephus, with great fear we went inside the tomb and found no body... no body at all, we ran away to tell the Captain about it... but he was speaking with some priests outside the praetorian, the Captain was mad to know we weren't at our posts, as we started to explain what happened he was deeply concerned, saying "we need to know more about this Jesus", the priests got upset and started to rebuke us telling us that we were liars, we said that we weren't liars, the body wasn't there and an angel did this!"

- Longinus: "This Jesus is truly the Son of God, then what happened?"

- Lacius: "The Captain allowed us to go and tell the some other priests what happened, we went there and after a while we were in front of what they call the Sanhedrin, we told everything that I just said to you... first they said that we were liars, then we replied we are soldiers of Rome, we don't lie; then they started to deliberate among themselves and after a while they told us to keep quiet about it and they were prepared to purchased our silence, Josephus arranged the payoff, actually I was still a little shock by everything that happened, I haven't even counted whatever money they gave us... do you believe me Longinus? do you believe what I'm saying?"

- Longinus: "Yes Lacius I believe you..."

- Lacius: "What should we do my friend this man was Holy! I mean, an angel stealing His body? What shall I do now Longinus? this is no good for me and my family, we will never enter the afterlife!"

- Longinus: "Fear not my friend; remember what he said when we were nailing Him...?

- Lacius: "No...What did He said then?"

- Longinus: "Father forgive them they do not know what they do."

- Lacius: "Yes that's right, He did say that!... Well, I think I should just use this money"

- Longinus: "That money is tied to the truth they want to hide, about what really happened to Jesus... give it back!"

- Lacius: "Really?... didn't Jesus forgave us?"

- Longinus: "Yes he did my friend, but that money is cursed because is buying your silence so that they would hide their offenses to God, they feel good because they have bought you, they have bought a voice that witness a miracle done by God, do you truly want this on you?"

- Lacius: "You're right!... You convinced me my friend, thanks..."

It really was a weird and sad at the same time, an awesome time for me to have met the Son of God in such a gruesome way... It's been a couple of months already and my Captain called me to meet his friend.

- Captain: "Longinus this is Cornelius, stationed in Cafarnaum truly a gentleman and a Hero of Rome..."

- Cornelius: "Please Antipas stop the praise; I'm just your friend."

- Longinus: "What?...Antipas? That's you name Captain?..."

- Captain: "Longinus, if you tell anybody I will find the most hellish post out there and give it to you for a whole month!"

- Longinus: "Don't worry Captain Antipas my lips are sealed..."

- Cornelius: "You got to be kidding me? Your troop didn't know your name? ha,ha,ha,ha... Wow, Antipas... you really need to lighten up a little bit... What was your name again soldier?

- Longinus: "Longinus... I apologize Sir, I'm very pleased to meet you...I've been waiting anxiously your arrival Sir, we need to know more about this Jesus."

- Cornelius: "Please call me Cornelius."

He sat down and explained that when he got to Cafarnaum, he use to hate everything about that town, hate everything about everything... Cornelius explained to us that his only son has died in Rome in an accident when he was trying to calm an uprising here in "Jew country", he felt overwhelmed by despair by not being there with his boy, he felt lost and deceive by Rome because Tiberius prolonged the service to 20 years, if it remained like it was he would've been at home and his death prevailed.

- Cornelius: "For a whole year I felt much anger inside poisoning me to my very soul, during those times I've made the lives out of everybody under my command miserable, I made the Jews miserable, there was nothing inside... a big nothing! I was riding my horse coming back from some military exercise and I saw this young Jewish boy walking around crying, I approach him to know what was going on, for my surprise the boy reminded me a lot of my young son! It was amazing how this Jewish boy look so much to my son... He said that his father just died, when I asked about his family he said that his mother died when he was born that he didn't had no one else in this world... I demounted my horse I cried like a bay with him, and I asked him if he wanted to be my family because I didn't had any family as well, I said to him that I had a son but died, after that my wife was crazy and had to leave her behind with her family because my duty as a soldier was calling me, I need a son and you need a father if you want we could be a family to each other, the boy cried more put his little hand in my cheek and said:

- "Yes! we could be a family...!"

It was the most beautiful day of that year, I felt I was been born again... Four years later Ignatius my boy, was really ill... spend a lot in doctors but my boy didn't recover, day by day he was worst and worst and my life was leaving me each step he took to the grave, luckily for me I heard about Jesus from some Jew that saw my situation.

- "Commander, there is a solution to the illness of your boy... please go and speak to the prophet Jesus from Nazareth, He is outside of Cafarnaum teaching and healing the people, they say that he throws out demons with authority and they obey, even they say that at some wedding He turn water into wine as the wedding ran short of it."

- Cornelius: "Really? If He does what you say and Commands even Demons to go out of possess people, then He is a Holy man and me and my house are not worthy He steps His feet in it."

- "Well Commander I'll truly hate for that boy of yours to die today."

I quickly made up my mind, I went out to find Jesus in order for Him to save my boy's life, fortunate for me as I was about to leave the town, he was coming in.

- Cornelius: "Lord, my boy is lying at home paralyzed, suffering dreadfully."

- Jesus: "I will come and cure him."

- Cornelius: "Lord, I am not worthy to have you enter under my roof; only say the word and my boy will be heal for I too am a person subject to authority, with soldiers subject to me. And I say to one, 'Go,' and he goes; and to another, 'Come here,' and he comes; and to my slave, 'Do this,' and he does it."

- Jesus: "Amen, I say to you, in no one in Israel have I found such faith. I say to you, many will come from the east and the west, and will recline with Abraham, Isaac, and Jacob at the banquet in the kingdom of heaven, but the children of the kingdom will be driven out into the outer darkness, where there will be wailing and grinding of teeth."

-Jesus: "You may go; as you have believed, let it be done for you."

I came back home and it was like He said, my boy was there smiling at me, he called me "Father, a man name Jesus said to me to rise and wait for you, my illness it's gone!"...Praise the God of the Jews for Jesus the prophet, He came and healed my boy at the same time, what a display of power! I was crying, hugging my son thanking God for Jesus when the Jew that told me about Jesus came in and marveled...

- "Isn't God wonderful my friend, I told you that Jesus could cure him."

- Cornelius: "Yes Stephen...you did."

- Stephen: "Yes Commander, I have to leave you because I'm going to Jerusalem, my whole family is moving there, but before I do, I need to leave you with what one of my cousin told me Jesus said in the mountain, I tell you He is wonderful and I hope it helps you from now on."

- Cornelius: " What is it Stephen?"

- Stephen: "He said:"

"Blessed are the poor in spirit, for theirs is the kingdom of heaven."
"Blessed are they who mourn, for they will be comforted."
"Blessed are the meek, for they will inherit the land."
"Blessed are they who hunger and thirst for righteousness, for they will be satisfied. "
"Blessed are the merciful, for they will be shown mercy."
"Blessed are the clean of heart, for they will see God."
"Blessed are the peacemakers, for they will be called children of God."
"Blessed are they who are persecuted for the sake of righteousness, for theirs is the kingdom of heaven."
"Blessed are you when they insult you and persecute you and utter every kind of evil against you (falsely) because of me."
"Rejoice and be glad, for your reward will be great in heaven. Thus they persecuted the prophets who were before you."
"You are the salt of the earth. But if salt loses its taste, with what can it be seasoned? It is no longer good for anything but to be thrown out and trampled underfoot."
"You are the light of the world. A city set on a mountain cannot be hidden."
"Nor do they light a lamp and then put it under a bushel basket; it is set on a lampstand, where it gives light to all in the house Just so, your light must shine before others, that they may see your good deeds and glorify your heavenly Father."
"Do not think that I have come to abolish the law or the prophets. I have come not to abolish but to fulfill."
- Stephen: "He came to fulfill as He was saying, He is healing people and showing them the Mercy of Heaven, I wish that I could follow Him right now but after my family gets established in Jerusalem I'll follow him strong; I hope that knowing this wisdom gives you an edge to go about your business Commander, Mercy has been given to you, so please live like you appreciate God's Mercy."

- Cornelius: "Thank you and I tell you, today is the start of a new me..."

- Cornelius: "Stephen went away as I was marveling at God, on how He remembered me and showed me His Love, I came here to learned that not only did Jesus died on the cross but my friend Stephen got stoned by the priests of this town, only because he believed that Jesus Resurrected."

- Longinus: "Well, the Captain and I can tell you right now that an angel came out of the heavens, while a couple of my soldier friends remained posted outside of His tomb, and they say that an angel rolled back the stone, much later the body was gone... I could tell you that this story is true, because the captain knows that his men don't lie to him."

- Captain: "That's true Cornelius...it happened exactly as Longinus is telling you."

We were amazed of how Jesus had so much power and at the same time puzzled, we needed to find more information about Jesus and see exactly how we needed to proceed, Cornelius returned to his town and the Captain (Antipas...ha,ha,ha...), stayed being our Captain.

It wasn't a year since Jesus died; the growing pain about me killing Jesus took a toll on me, so deserted my troop and flee, I had to find answers about Jesus... I wanted to see Cornelius again but I was told that he moved, by the word of mouth he was staying in the sea city of Caesarea, so I went there. It has been years since I've seen Cornelius, I've wonder what he had found about the Son of God... after a couple of weeks traveling I finally got to Caesarea, I started to ask around and see if they knew about a Centurion named Cornelius, it wasn't hard, since he was popular, I got there at night I thought that going to the army station there wasn't a good idea because of my desertion, besides a soldier of his size is not going to be there at night, I entered the city and immediately somebody knew, I knocked on the door I was directed to and it was him.

- Longinus: "Cornelius?"

- Cornelius: "Who wants to know?"

- Longinus: "It's me Longinus! Do you remember? Antipas, Jerusalem... Jesus?

- Cornelius: "Oh sweet God...hello my friend, how are you...please come in... it's been long since we last saw each other..."

- Longinus: "Yes my friend, it is awesome to see you and yes, it's been long."

- Cornelius: "So how it's Antipas? What brings you here my dear friend?"

- Longinus: "Antipas is fine, his service is up soon and mine ended a few weeks ago, now... I opted to stay out of the military for good and focus in knowing more about Jesus, this is why I came here."

- Cornelius: "Really? Well you've come to the right place my friend, I need to tell you everything... I'm a Christian..."

- Longinus: "A Christian... what is that?"

- Cornelius: "That's how everybody calls Jesus... the Christ, and his followers are being called Christians."

- Longinus: "So you're a follower?"

- Cornelius: "Well the apostles use more the word: believers... so yes I follow Jesus; He's my Lord and my Savior."

- Longinus: "I don't understand... Apostles? Your Lord and Savior?"

- Cornelius: "Listen, one day an angel appeared to me in a vision and told me that my prayers were answered and that I needed to find Peter, he was staying in Joppa at Simon's house. I sent two of my men and a soldier to look for Peter, when they found him he agreed to come to my house, there... I was with my entire family and told him about my vision, then he started telling his vision: He was hungry and wished to eat, and while they were making preparations he fell into a trance.

He saw heaven opened and something resembling a large sheet coming down, lowered to the ground by its four corners. In it were all the earth's four-legged animals and reptiles and the birds of the sky. A voice said to him, "Get up, Peter. Slaughter and eat. "But Peter said, "Certainly not, sir. For never have I eaten anything profane and unclean." The voice spoke to him again, a second time, "What God has made clean, you are not to call profane." and this happened three times, and then the object was taken up into the sky. He acknowledged that God was calling all of His children including non-Jews as he saw the Holy Spirit descending into our hearts; me and my family got baptized that day, now we have Jesus the Son of the Living God as our Lord and Savior, we got the gift of the Holy Spirit."

- Longinus: "What??"

- Cornelius: "Look, there are no words to describe exactly how the Mercy of God works within you, after Jesus healed my son back in Cafarnaum I changed forever, I was an angry man, a destructive one... my wife lost in madness and my Son died in an accident, after I found another opportunity to be happy with my boy he was doomed to die until Jesus healed him, from that day I committed myself to the only God, the one true God that the Jews worship day and night, I've committed myself be merciful like God was Merciful to me through Jesus His only begotten Son, He took our offenses, He took our sins and destroyed the chains that bound us to death... God in His eternal Mercy saw my good deeds and called me to become one of His, I got baptized in water, Peter the apostle prayed to Jesus so I could get the Holy Spirit of God sealed in my heart... and my entire soul was filled by the sweet fire of the most High, and now my life as change from night to day, His Mercy is within me and Mercy I've showed not because I could, but because Jesus loves me."

- Longinus: "Where can I find this apostle...? Peter? I want what you have, please tell me Cornelius..."

- Cornelius: "He went to Joppa afterwards, but he wasn't staying there because of the Good news of Jesus, Peter told me that he needed to go to Rome so maybe he's there... listen, it's a dangerous time right now to become a Christian, there's evil within some people, my friend Stephen died because He was a witness of the cause, you shall stay here tonight my friend so you can rest..."

- Longinus: "Thank you my friend for your hospitality... I will leave first light in the morning... I really need to find the apostles so I could have what you have, but also..."

- Cornelius: "What my friend? What troubles your heart?"

- Longinus: "I have to show you this..."

- Cornelius: "A spear?"

- Longinus: (Crying) "With this I opened the chest of the Son of God, Blood and Water came down from his side...I did recovered my blind eye with it, as you can see there's still blood there..."

Cornelius quickly drop to his knees and shouted "I'm not worthy to stand in front of His Royal Blood", I cried more and more and told Cornelius that I was having this recurring dream every now and then, that even though after the dream ends I have no guilt a few days later guilt was there stronger than before... I need to find the apostles and tell me exactly what to do with it.

- Cornelius: "I think my dear friend that you are destined for great things, I hear what you are saying and I totally understand, tomorrow you shall leave to Rome seeking the apostles, I have a friend that might get you some help, but please be careful... danger is everywhere!"

Next day I thanked my friend for everything and I took the road to Rome, there wasn't one road to Rome specifically, so I took a boat to Antioch bordering all the coast, even though I was heading north and Rome was to the west, I was sure that a big city like Antioch should have a boat more direct to Rome since Caesarea didn't had any at the time, but God was directing me straight to His Mercy.

After days in that boat finally we got to Antioch, it was easy to find Christians, as I found a man called Simeon or better said, as he found me! I was resting below a tree with the sign of the Christians in the sand, the sign of a fish... Cornelius showed me this in Caesarea to avoid problems, Simeon came and acknowledged that I was a Christian then we went to a secluded area and there, I was introduced to Paul.

- Longinus: "Hello, my name is Longinus..."

- Paul: "Pardon my manners but are you a Christian?"

- Longinus: "No... Unfortunately I'm not..."

- Paul: "Are you seeking the crucified?"

- Longinus: "You see... I was the one who killed him... I killed Jesus in the cross..."

- Paul: "Yes you did, but so did I and the entire world, Jesus came as the sacrifice foretold in prophecies to the children of Israel for them and the entire world."

- Longinus: "You don't understand, I was the Roman soldier who thrust his spear into His Holy side... much Water and Blood came down and took my blindness away... I feel every now and then so much guilt, even though I know I was forgiven... it hurts so much!"

- Paul: " I hear you Longinus and you have seen the mystery of Mercy working for many, before Jesus came into this world, men were chained to death and this chains were sin, we were all slaves to sin and the wages of sin is death, but the gift of God is eternal life in Christ Jesus our Lord... do you want that for you Longinus?"

- Longinus: "Yes I accept Jesus as my Lord and Savior and I truly repent of all my bad deeds."

- Paul: "Wonderful my child... let's take you to the water, to baptize you."

We went to the Orontes river and there I was baptized in the name of the Father, the Son and the Holy Spirit... all of my sins were forgiven as I saw the Holy Spirit descend upon me He showed me each and every sin I had, the slaughter of many in battle, the assassination of many throughout the Empire's conquest, all of the Lust I had for both women and men, this sins and many more were shown to me in a vision and destroyed with Holy fire like a rolls on fire... the only one that I thirst to be gone for good, was me thrusting my lance unto Jesus, but the Holy Spirit told me that I was forgiven and I had to suffer the same pain as Jesus side until the day I'll be beheaded in Cappadocia."

- Longinus: "Now... I have re-born again!"

- Paul: "Isn't it wonderful how you look at things now and how you use to look at things before?"

- Longinus: "I thank you my Sweet Jesus for your Mercy, which has recover for us spiritual health and nurture us with Your Love, Thank you Father for Your Son!"

- Paul: "From now on we must be brave and courageous for the sake of His Kingdom, you had guilt over the thrust you took on Jesus side, but it had to be that way in order for us to get clean... the Mystery of Mercy is this: Blood and Water that burst into the wind for the salvation of many; we all have the opportunity to get salvation through Him, but most prefer the ways of the world and it's wickedness, it had to be you Longinus to open The Treasure that became flesh and dwell among us, Mercy personified, The Son of God! Now my brother you should go to Cappadocia and suffer so that many believe!"

- Longinus: "You knew what was going on?"

- Paul: "The Holy Spirit is also with me and He showed me all of this before you even put a foot at Caesarea, please do know my brother in Christ, that not only you have blood in your hands, I persecuted many that believe in Him and also watch them died, I personally persecuted them until Jesus revealed Himself to me."

- Longinus: "Himself to you? What a great honor!"

- Paul: "Indeed, I was walking to Damascus in order to bring back to Jerusalem whoever was a believer of Jesus when suddenly a huge light blinded me, I fell to the ground and a voice calls my name: "Saul, Saul, why are you persecuting me?" I demanded to know who was He: "I am Jesus, whom you are persecuting." In an instant I thought what Stephen said in the Sanhedrin was true, when he finally said: "I see heaven open and the Son of Man standing at the right hand of God." that was his doom... They stoned Him and I didn't do anything to stop it, I persecuted a lot of people taking them out of their homes to be imprisoned, that is with me forever until the day I die, but suffering a little bit in order to gain heaven is a good price to pay; Longinus you need to leave the lance here for the sake of the church so many would believe, and you need to pray for the conversion of many and fight with the armor of God the spirit of iniquity in Cappadocia."

- Longinus: "The armor of God?"

- Paul: "Faith, The Holy Spirit, the Word of God, Jesus Flesh and Blood and when you get all this beasts coming from the depths of hell out to get you, remember that in the name of Jesus every knee shall kneel... talking about His flesh and blood, we need to start the banquet... come and participate my brother, there you shall leave the Spear to venerate."

Paul then put his hands in my head and prayed for me, The Holy Spirit was burning my heart with Divine Love... I wasn't surprised that he knew about the spear even before I could tell him, The Holy Spirit revealed everything to Paul and I Loved that from Holy Spirit, because He reveals the Word of God and show us how to pray, what to do, where to go and what to say, through Him... Jesus was revealed to us in such a clear and calm state; I gave the spear to Barnabas so it could be displayed to all, I came to the banquet and it was something beyond words, I was seeing angels there everywhere and Paul celebrated the banquet, He said the blessing prayer in order that the bread he was holding could become Jesus flesh, Paul filled our mouths with it, immediately I was in a trance, I taken to the mount of olives and there I saw Jesus suffering for all men, I could see the weight of all the sin did by men since the beginning of God's creation, to the present where we were, and all the sin from the future...

The future was more harder because men were lovers of themselves, in the future most of the Christians didn't love thy brothers, they loved themselves... in the mind of my Lord these were lukewarm Christians, that's when His sweat blood and fell to the ground, He cried: "Father, if it is possible, let this cup pass from me; yet, not as I will, but as you will." He was referring about lukewarm people... millions of them!

Then an angel came down and comforted Him, that angel looked into my eyes and immediately I was back into the banquet, when Paul said the blessing and gave the Chalice of salvation to us so we always remember His Passion, I took His Blood freely, again I was taken to Jerusalem I was seeing myself participating in the beating, laughing in the coronation, and finally putting the spear into His side... all the roads and passages in Jerusalem were tainted with His Holy Blood, and they Knew they were killing someone from Heaven and didn't care, because the Pharisees, scribes and some other people were children of the devil... even though I was forgiven it was hard for me to see my participation, then I saw the thief crucified with Jesus and he told me: "I prayed for your conversion Longinus and the Lord has you in His plans, now go to Cappadocia soldier in Christ... for the Kingdom now you must fight through prayer... A light was floating beside Him and I knew somebody was there, I asked who was with him.

- Jesus: "It is me Longinus... It is me, Jesus."

- Longinus: "My Sweet God... forgive me, I didn't know you were the Son of the living God."

- Jesus: "It was written, no bone on me would be crushed... I forgave you a long time ago, from now on I want you to live in prayer and be an example in Cappadocia, there you shall be my witness."

- Longinus: "I'm your soldier my Lord and my God, I will do what you ask of me."

Right there, the vision ended and I was back at the Banquet, afterwards Paul told me...

- Paul: "You shall rest now my brother, your path starts when you set foot on your way to Cappadocia..."

It was morning and everything was different, the sun, the birds, the clouds, the air in my lungs, I've never seen or felt such beautiful and magnificent creations by Almighty Father up in heaven, those things were of no relevance... no relevance at all by old Longinus, last night I was born again, I'm the creation that God envision when He created me, it'll be a long path for me to be worthy enough, but with my own strength there's nothing I could do or say that could make me worthy of His Love, I'm sure that through Jesus Mercy I could enter heaven.

Next morning Barnabas came for me...

- Barnabas: "Hello my brother, good morning... I've came for you as we are about to start the morning prayers before breakfast."

We started morning prayers and it was all beautiful, we read a Isaiah and we concentrated in one piece the prophet said:

"For just as from the heavens the rain and snow come down And do not return there till they have watered the earth, making it fertile and fruitful, Giving seed to him who sows and bread to him who eats, So shall my word be that goes forth from my mouth; It shall not return to me void, but shall do my will, achieving the end for which I sent it."

Oh my Sweet God may Your Word stays with us, every word...forever! I want more of it, I'm thirsty my Lord, I'm thirsty of Your Mercy, come my Lord, come to me your soldier, your servant, your slave!

Before we got into the morning prayers I was told to wash my right hand, we will take the Flesh and Blood of Jesus before our journey, Barnabas explained to me that we are rushing things for the sake of spreading the good news of the Gospel, he explained that because the church of Jesus is being persecuted, we needed to be brief as danger was in the air, today we will take the Holy Flesh in our right hand reverently and with our right hand take the Holy flesh directly into our mouths...

Last night we all took the Holy flesh in the mouth as in the original Banquet took place, with Jesus and the Apostles.

- Longinus: "I'm not worthy Barnabas to take it in my murderous hands."

- Barnabas: "No one is my brother, no one is worthy... not even angels can touch Jesus, as the Son of God is too Holy for anybody outside The Holy Trinity and His own Mother; but danger is coming for us, as the church sometimes has no rest from the enemies controlled by the devil."

- Longinus: "I understand..."

We took the Holy flesh of Christ in our right hands and straight to our mouths taking all fragments in leaving nothing to fall... I did felt my Sweet Jesus going in and traveled throughout all my flesh, ligaments, mind until He got inside my soul... what a wonderful and special feeling, my Lord has gave me a lot by forgiving my sins and giving me tremendous amounts of His Mercy, my heart is burning more than the sun of any desert I've been, it was indeed amazing Mercy that touched my unworthy heart. After the banquet and prayers we took a small breakfast, my brothers were preparing to leave to Tarsus and I was preparing to go to Cappadocia.

- Barnabas: "My brother Longinus it's been awesome knowing you, I hope we could see each other again and hear that all Cappadocia has been converted by your way of life through Christ."

- Longinus: "Thank you Barnabas, I wish that too..."

- Paul: "My brother I will pray for you so you could present a good battle..."

- Longinus: "A good battle?"

- Paul: "That is correct, you are going where regarding corruption... all things imaginable you will see, but you have the Holy Spirit, He will speak through your lips and teach you right from wrong, He'll give you strength so you could persevere in faith, pray for Mercy for the conversion of all men, pray for us and your enemies... so we could be washed in the Blood and Water that gush each day from the side of Jesus, the same Blood and Water that regained your sight, know that His Mercy can be eaten... take His Flesh and Blood with love and devotion knowing the bread and wine are not actually bread and wine, but food out the depths of His Mercy, repent of your sins each day with true conversion, seek humility so you can get to the doors of Heaven, know that the Word of God is your weapon, when in doubt say His Holy Name: Jesus, so you could break away from all evil, because every knee shall kneel upon hearing His beautiful name and His name has all the power necessary to create and destroy.

- Paul: Never forget all I have tell you today soldier, these are your weapons now, rely on them to defeat evil in the name of His Kingdom."

- Longinus: "I will not forget..."

- Paul: "So long my brother, may the peace of the Lord be with you and His Mercy be your refuge forever."

- Barnabas: "Peace Longinus, peace be with you..."

- Longinus: "Peace."

With tears in my eyes we went our separate ways, the blessing of the Lord though the lips of brother Paul were beautiful and gave great hope, in each town I went on the way to Cappadocia, I did find Christians and I did find persecution, it was tough because of the Holy banquet... we had to do it in hiding and I dislike the idea of taking the Holy Flesh in my right hand, but it was fine because there will be a time when the church will not persecuted so heavily and we could go back to the original banquet and taking His Flesh in our mouths.

I was a Roman citizen, the early heavy persecution at the time was done by Christ's own people, the Jews; sometimes it did went further than only a Jew problem when they agitated the pagans, the Jews were calling it "the way", the pagans were calling us Christians, but that wasn't a shocker because I've been hearing that for long, others the claimed that we were agitators, corruptors, etc... I did like "the way", because it reflected what Jesus said himself:

- "I am the way and the truth and the life. No one comes to the Father except through me."

Yes, He is the way... the way that we must take in order to be truly free, some people think that they will see the Father... but the door has been shut for the people that doesn't recognize Him as the Lord of Lords, King of Kings, and the only begotten Son from Almighty Father... Jesus I am your soldier! I am the soldier of Jesus my Lord; I cried freely out of joy like a little boy, yes I hunger for thee my Sweet King... I am truly your servant... Suddenly, I get this awful and asphyxiating smell behind me.

- Ha, ha, ha, ha... so now you are a soldier of Love?

- Longinus: "Get behind me Satan you evil and despicable murderer."

- "Murderer? ha,ha,ha,ha..."

Then he showed me all the people that I've killed during my service in the military, all the people that I did slash their throats or break their skulls, as they were all chanting:

- "We will see you in hell and we'll feast with you..."

- Longinus: "In the name of Jesus my Lord I cast you into hell..."

With a loud voice they all disappeared, but I knew that this was only the beginning of things to come...

- Well done!

- Longinus: "Who are you?"

- "I'm your guardian angel Longinus."

- Longinus: "Guardian angel?"

- "Yes soldier, Jesus the Son of Almighty God, gave Himself as sacrifice for the salvation of men and will not forsake you in this war, you are not alone... Give yourself to Jesus more and more every day and try always to seek His Mercy by prayer, sacrifice and being an example to all."

- Longinus: "All the praise and glory are His forever!"

After that exchange, the angel disappeared; I understood that the angel was there the whole time as this was allowed to happen as a test, Oh! My Sweet Jesus please don't ever leave me on my own, without you I'm nothing! Several days passed by and I was getting near to Cappadocia, the angel of the Lord took me to a high place and showed me where I was going.

- "Look Longinus, there's Cappadocia."

I saw a region full of idols everywhere, demons running everywhere as fire from hell governs the whole place.

- "That's what God wants you to be at, that's where the real battle is going to take place."

- Longinus: "I'm ready to give my life for the sake of the good news of the Gospel, through prayer, sacrifice and example... Jesus will win this battle for me as I'm an incompetent and unworthy servant of the Lord."

- "Rely at all costs on Jesus Mercy and you'll be fine."

The angel took me back where I was before, he gave me the Holy Flesh as he took it from Peter the apostle hands for me. The Lord sees my spiritual needs and He fulfills them. It was night already as I was entering a town in Cappadocia also called Caesarea.

Through the darkness of the city I could see the eyes of all this demons hidden in the darkness, hissing and cursing... but they didn't dare to come near as the angel of the lord lighted my way all throughout the town, we got to the house of somebody familiar to me.

- Longinus: "Aphrodisius?"

- Aphrodisius: "Hello Longinus, I've been waiting for you... peace be with you!"

I quickly hugged my old friend from my military days, it was good to see a familiar face...

- Longinus: "Peace of the Lord be with you too Aphrodisius, you don't Know how good is to see you again!"

- Aphrodisius: "Likewise, I've been waiting for long to welcome you to this hellish town my friend, I've been praying for a brother full with The Holy Spirit to get here fast, all this demons are taking a toll on me."

- Longinus: "Aphrodisius, do not despair my brother, if you do... then the battle is lost!"

- Aphrodisius: "Yes your right, your right... I'm sorry, I know that it's not you or anybody that will win this fight, the only one that could, is our Savior and Lord Jesus."

- Longinus: "It is good to see you again... now tell me all I need to know about what's going on in this whole region."

Cappadocia was overrun by wickedness, as my good friend was telling me, it's cities full of idols, people worshiping other gods than the One we serve; authorities were the instigating factor letting people go to their doom, they were promoting it and sometimes with joy, as they did their celebrations that ended in large feasts and mass orgies, were all sorts of abominations occurred in the light of day.

- Longinus: "We need to start right away!"

- Aphrodisius: "What do you think we should do?"

- Longinus: "Like you said, we need to win this war here in Cappadocia by realizing that we are not the ones winning it, that we are weak and worthless, we need our Commander so He could win ordering us what to do, we need our Lord Jesus to take this city by storm... I remembered when we killed Him in the cross that Blood and Water came down from His side, through the wound on His side we need to convert whoever that might want to listen to the truth, the ones that are His and this can only be through His Powerful Mercy that gush from His side... our course of action is to pray, we need His help all day, all night, whenever... but we have to ask His Mercy for all of our brothers too spreading the word, so come Aphrodisius let or lives be a constant prayer, a constant sacrifice, a constant suffering... So it begins in the Name of the Father, the Son and the Holy Spirit."

We started praying the Lord's Prayer and no one teach that to us before, nobody ever said tell us about this incredible and powerful prayer... The Holy Spirit took over; He showed us the prayer and a scene where Jesus took the time to teach His disciples.

- "Lord, teach us to pray just as John taught his disciples."

- Jesus: "When you pray, say: Father, hallowed be your name, your kingdom come."

- "Give us each day our daily bread and forgive us our sins for we ourselves forgive everyone in debt to us, and do not subject us to the final test."

And He went on and said to them:

- Jesus: "Suppose one of you has a friend to whom he goes at midnight and says, 'Friend, lend me three loaves of bread, for a friend of mine has arrived at my house from a journey and I have nothing to offer him, and he says in reply from within, 'Do not bother me; the door has already been locked and my children and I are already in bed. I cannot get up to give you anything.'"

- Jesus: "And I tell you, ask and you will receive; seek and you will find; knock and the door will be opened to you. For everyone who asks, receives; and the one who seeks, finds; and to the one who knocks, the door will be opened."

The vision went out and we were ending the Golden prayer and suddenly all the darkness and demons that dare to be around our house were cast into hell with tremendous Power, light embraced us as the ground opened right at the door of the house, we were able to see as the door opened, how some of this creatures were cast into hell, they were falling into the abyss and even though they could fly, they were froze by Christ's power...

Some were just thrown into the abyss, but the ones that dared to go near our house were chained there forever, as the ground started to close I could see millions of people inside the abyss, millions! They were being tortured over and over again... it was horrible; afterwards, the angel of the Lord told us both:

- "It was a sad thing that men were falling into the abyss day and night!"

- Longinus: "Why men are going there in the first place?"

- "The Abyss of fire was created for satan and his rebels, there... fire will consumed them for all eternity, hell wasn't constructed for men, Almighty Father wanted to bless men, but they chose a life of wickedness and all type of pleasures of the flesh... God wanted man to be happy, but men chose the trap of sin... and by their horrible sins they are marching into hell. The good thing is that the Lamb of God freed them from the chains of sin, the King of Kings paid a huge price for all men with His precious Blood in Jerusalem and all who are marching to hell can go back to God's grace by His Mercy, all who asks for His Mercy with a true, sincere and broken spirit shall receive the Treasure of the Heavens, which is His powerful Mercy."

The angel of the Lord then disappeared, we prayed the whole night until morning light, after our prayers were over we took a little meal and went out to see the city, see how people lived and meet a few Christians along the way.

A few years passed by, we prayed for our brothers everywhere around the world, we prayed for the conversion of men, we prayed so that all of our faith grows more and more, we prayed for the ones that believe in the good news of the Gospel of the Lord, we preached His Mercy to all who wanted to hear His beautiful name, sometimes He healed the sick through our hands, sometimes did miracles here and there through prayer and fasting, and it was all He... thank God that He did this things as I Longinus were His worthless soldier incapable of doing anything without Him.

One day I'd preached against an idol placed outside of a house, as people came to ask the owner's son... about numbers, fortune telling... typical of hellish beings.

- Longinus: "Do not seek nothing outside of the Truth and Love of the One true God, who sent His only begotten Son Jesus and raised Him from the dead so we could have eternal life in Him, turn away from your wickedness and repent now that the Kingdom of God is within reach, accept Jesus as your Lord and Savior and get baptized for the forgiveness of your sins and you shall receive the gift of the Holy Spirit!!"

- "Shut up monk! We are trying to hear what this child has to say."

- Longinus: "I Bind you in the name of the Holy Spirit, Kneel before the Holy Cross so that the Lord shall dispose of you, you wicked being... leave this child now I say and you... sculpture of madness and deceit, shall crumble before us and disappeared within the wind."

The child then fell to the ground and with a loud voice the demon came out of his body and was thrown into the lake of fire, at the same time the idol crumbled before our very eyes and the wind took it like a sand in a storm, everybody was amazed by the Power of our Lord Jesus, the child was thankful as he said to his father that he was trapped in darkness for so long, he thought that it was going to be like that forever and now he could see the light of a new day all thanks to Jesus, that day many converted.

One day we were at the Holy banquet as soon as I took His Flesh in my mouth, I fell into ecstasy... the angel of the Lord took me to a high place in Cappadocia and pointed me to Jerusalem, my eyes turned to the city were we killed my Lord, my eyesight traveled there in an instant and saw all the apostles gathered around somebody that was asleep... a woman; I was given the knowledge that all the apostles, traveled great lengths in order to be there that day to witness it all... then the heavens were opened, the angel and me threw ourselves to the ground in adoration as we could see Jesus beside His Father and the Holy Spirit... Almighty Father said with a voice that created the most beautiful flowers I have ever seen throughout the whole world:

- "COME FORTH."

The woman as she started to be lifted from the ground to heaven, I thought to myself "I've seen that woman before", back in the day she had swollen eyes because of my Lord Jesus at the cross, it's the Mother of my Lord Jesus! She had her eyes closed as I understood that she didn't die, that she was only asleep... all angels in heaven were singing: "Blessed is She who believed in the Lord, Blessed is She who said yes." It was beyond words, nothing that I could say can describe the joy of the Heavens as she went inside God's palace, then the heavens closed and the angel told me.

- "It fulfilled the joy of the Korahites when she said, YES to the Lord: **"Listen, my daughter, and understand; pay me careful heed. Forget your people and your father's house, that the king might desire your beauty. He is your Lord; honor Him, daughter of Tyre. Then the richest of the people will seek your favor with gifts. All glorious is the King's daughter as she enters, her raiment threaded with gold; In embroidered apparel she is led to the King. The maids of her train are presented to the King. They are led in with glad and joyous acclaim; they enter the palace of the King. The throne of your fathers your sons will have; you shall make them princes through all the land. I will make your name renowned through all generations; thus nations shall praise you forever."**
- Longinus: "She did suffer all the way to the cross with her Son."

- "Yes her pain was great, inflicted right through her heart! And it's sad that most will turn away from her, even though she could seek favors for them, as it is written that she could get those from the Lord. There are those who even will say awful things about her, but that's war... divide and conquer, right soldier? the church will be divided in the future and all of this will be done by men... not by God, but there is nothing man can do against God's plans, because His will always get done, the enemies of the church will try to erase her, forget her... but how can you erase from your life the Mother of your Savior? How can you erase her example? Even though she is the Queen of Mercy, she is the slave of the King of Mercy and desires the salvation of all men."

- Longinus: "What about those that will follow Her steps into the King's palace, who are they?"

- "Those are the ones that will say yes to the Lord as she did, the ones that will preserve themselves pure for the King of Kings, they will get many souls for Him."

- Longinus: "What about her sons? The ones that shall get the thrones...?"

- "John the apostle stood in front of Jesus at the cross and Jesus said: "Son behold your Mother... Mother behold your Son and from that day the disciple took her into his home." The apostle's home was referring to the church and the apostle is a priest, every priest needs to stand in front of the cross and let Jesus tell them precisely that, so all of them can take Mary into their homes, she will be a Mother to the priest and the priest a son to Mary, it is written that her only desire for her sons is for them to do whatever Jesus tells them."

- Longinus: "Mary is her name, the Mother of my Sweet Lord?"

- "Yes, understand that those who finds her, finds life and wins favor from the Lord... understand that you'll need all the tools at your disposal in order to get Mercy from our Lord Jesus, and that's the favor that you'll get... Mercy and what is her Mercy? Nothing more than the Blessed fruit of her womb... Jesus."

- Longinus: "My Mother died when I came into this world, I was raised by men alone... but now I know I have a Mother that looks after me before my lovely King."

- "Well said soldier."

Then he took me where I was before, all of my brothers were praying for me, when I got back they were all marveled by all the things the angel said and showed me, I told my brothers the vision is for them to use in prayers, Aphrodisius told me it was true as he was once with all of the apostles back in Jerusalem and they used to refer to Mary as their Mother when they spoke about the Lord's Mother, we all concluded that yes, our Lord is giving us His own Mother to His workers, how Lovely is our Lord!

A week later I was walking alone outside of town when I got ambushed by many demons, in my mind I prayed to the Lord saying: "My Lord this is so easy for you! Use my hands for the battle, do not let me do this myself because I'm weak and worthless, with your Love, I'm your soldier."

- "Today is the day monk! We are going to get you... we outnumbered you by the dozens there's nothing you could do!"

- Longinus: "If the Lord wants me to fall today, I am His slave... I'm His soldier that wouldn't dare to move, until I get His command!"

- "You pathetic and murderous monk... you're not getting salvation as you stink with sin... you will fall today!

In my mind I was just waiting for my orders as they started to punch, kick, and bite me; I closed my eyes slowly and saw in the sky: "Call formation, my child." I opened my eyes and said in the name of the Father, the Son and the Holy Spirit... A circle of angels surround them, they all wanted to flee... but they couldn't go anywhere as the angels bind them with their vision, one angel in an instant drew his sword and with out of this world speed wounded them all, they tried to hit him... 28 demons against one angel and they couldn't hit him once! The angel smiles while fighting the demos and told me: "Soldier! Close formation..."

I repeated in the name of the Father, the Son and the Holy Spirit, the wounds made by his sword grew and grew and turn them into dust statues, what a great battle...!

- "Don't worry your wounds shall heal tonight as your Mother will visit you..."

- Longinus: "You're different from all angels, who are you?"

- "I'm the archangel Saint Michael, I command my Lord's army of angels, I'm just a servant of who you serve... the Lamb of God."

He then folded his sword which by the way reflected stars, a weapon shinier than the sun...

- St. Michael: "Yes, this sword is beautiful and is made with the best material there is... the word of God! Please try and rest as an angel will take you back to the house."

Like a dream... all happened, but as I was carried to my bed by Aphrodisius, my wounds were deep and my bruises all swollen; I had the most horrendous night, I was burning up as all my injuries were drowning me in pain, every time I closed my eyes the same dream kept happening... me killing Jesus, mocking Him, punching Him over and over again, it seemed I was in that dream for a thousand years each time I close my eyes, until finally I broke out of that cycle by a visit.

- "Longinus, Longinus... is me your Mother!"

- Longinus: "Mother... Mother! Please forgive me, forgive me for killing your Son..."

- "I'm sorry Longinus I can't forgive you for what you did, you are a murderer, a criminal, an abomination, no one can forgive you, you are definitely going to hell!

I was froze in shock, yes my deeds are beyond repair and I truly deserve an eternity in hell... but something was off, something was definitely off, why she keep saying those things, I mean I get it... I know I'm not worthy of His Mercy in heaven, but what about this awful smell! What is going on?

- Longinus: "Oh! Mother that's why I pray, I pray because I'm not worthy... In the name of the Father, the Son and the Holy Spirit..."

- "NOOOOOOO!!"

It was the devil himself disguised as my Mother! Calling Christ's Mercy was brilliant as the devil's disguise melted and his true form was shown...

- Longinus: "I call upon the Mercy of the Lord; please Jesus with a little bit of Your Divine Power take this repugnant beast to hell..."

- You will never win monk! You will end up with me in hell!"

- Longinus: "I bind you by the power of the Holy Spirit and I throw you at the feet of Jesus so the Lord disposes of you as He pleases..."

- "NOOOOOOO!!"

I was drained as the devil disappeared, thank you Jesus for another battle in which you won, you always win and the will of the Father will be done every time... I praise You Sweet Lord. Then the Mother of Jesus appeared to me with two angels, she was radiant and beautiful as she was clothed with the sun, a cloud was at her feet with many flowers, one of the angels took me to bed as she was smiling.

- Longinus: "I'm sorry Mother for killing your Son, please forgive me..."

- Mary: "Don't worry my child you were forgiven a long time ago, rest my child and take this soup."

The Sweet Mother of my Lord sat down and gave me bits of a soup made out of depths of Her Son's Mercy, I couldn't stand each spoon, it was the Sweetest Thing ever! My wounds healed with the first taste, each spoon now was filling my soul with grace... it was awesome that Jesus my Lord sent His own Mother to take care of me, I was crying like a baby...

- Mary: "The joy out your tears are sincere and you have to be strong my child as you need to follow my Son."

- Longinus: "Yes Mother I will follow Him..."

- Mary: "He wants you to deny yourself pickup your cross and follow Him, don't be like so many thinking "I'm a good person", my child... do know that many has even done miracles in my Son's name and now are in hell, repent every day, pray, fast, do good deeds, make reparations and rely only in His Mercy. I'm your Mother and I will pray my Son's Mercy for you until we see each other again in heaven."

- Longinus: "I will follow Him, I will follow with my cross knowing who I'm following, I will show the world tremendous amounts of joy because I'm seeing my Lord before me, Jesus and I are walking to the death hill, where I shall be crucify with Him embracing His Mercy like the example given to us by the thief Dismas..."

My Sweet Mother then disappeared with a beautiful smile on her face; I was healed entirely and humbled by Her visit. The whole week passed by with continuous prayers and fasting as we were hearing the news about what our brothers are suffering for the sake of the Gospel, James was killed by King Agrippa I in Jerusalem after our Mother ascended, Peter was jailed to please the Jews, Paul was arrested in Caesarea and on his way to Rome for a hearing before the emperor, so many brothers dying by the hands of the Jews and the Romans all over, we were persecuted and sometimes had to hide, I knew that our time was coming to a close when the devil's followers here on earth revealed themselves.

I was praying in order to start some sort of a shakeup in this town, repeatedly we had idols being put together after the Holy Spirit destroyed them and that was a problem, so I prayed all day until the next morning... As the first ray of light hit the town I fell asleep and couldn't go to the morning prayers and the Holy banquet, the angel of the lord in my dreams showed me a battle.

- "Do you remember this battle soldier?"

- Longinus: "Yes, this was the battle were we took Barabbas prisoner..."

- "Yes, do you remember how your troops approach them?"

- Longinus: "We divide ourselves into four lines so we could attack all flanks, that way no one would try to escape."

- "That's what you need to do, take 3 more of your brothers go to the center of the town and preach as you walk away to your posts, there in the north post, south, east and west near the outside of the city... Start and end in the name of the Father, the Son and the Holy Spirit... make the Prayer of Prayers and all idols shall burn, tell them that anyone who doesn't want their house on fire need to throw out their idols. You need all of the strengths possible from the faith you have in our Lord's Mercy, since you missed the Holy Banquet, I took a piece of His flesh from the Banquet today... open your mouth soldier so it'll be filled with His Mercy!."

- Longinus: "I received my Lord and the angel disappeared."

We went to the center of the town and preach the good news of Jesus, we did exactly as the angel of the Lord told me, some people were skeptical, but many did believe and threw out the idols, we did the prayer and the idols got on fire, many houses burned and many lamented, after this lots of people converted as the idols screamed with the fire from the heavens; the authorities there noticed what happened, they were confused and shocked.

Days passed since this happened, news of the big conversion traveled fast, unfortunately all the way to Pontius Pilate ears, since I deserted the military after what I did to Jesus and the growing thirst for Him, I knew if they find me they could kill me on the spot. The dream about me killing Jesus over and over again started to come up again, this time it was more persistent with the difference that at the same side pierced by me to the Lord, the same side hurt me when I woke up, it was a sharp continuous pain that was persistent and I took it in the name of my Lord each day.

One day the angel of the Lord took me to a mountain; there he showed me the future regarding idols which I was fighting all over Cappadocia...

- "Idols will emerge once again much stronger than before in the distant future, right now you have done well my dear soldier, many have converted and soon you shall be Christ's witness in front of the Governor of Cappadocia, as we speak Pontius Pilate heard from you and now his assassins are preparing to take their horses soon and fulfilled their master's orders."

- Longinus: "More idols?"

- "Yes, the spirit of iniquity does not rest one bit, this time they're going to use flesh idols instead."

- Longinus: "Flesh idols?"

- "Yes soldier, this time they will use men."

- Longinus: "This can't be, it'll be harder to fight them as they need salvation as well."

- "They need to ask Jesus beautiful Mercy in order to be saved! But there's nothing that the enemy can do to tweak God's plan... Mercy shall be given through that side that you opened with your spear, if they trust the Water and Blood that gush from the heart of Jesus, even the hardest headed sinner should find salvation."

- Longinus: (Crying) "That is so beautiful, and you say that this is in the distant future?"

- "Yes Longinus."

- Longinus: "I guess that I shall see all of that from heaven as my time on this earth is coming to an end."

- "Well said, politicians, artists of all kind, doctors, kings, soldiers, and even men of God will be idols, worshipping the devil and the riches of this world..."

- Longinus: "Men of God?"

- "The devil shall have a little victory inside all the churches, they will preach against God tweaking everybody's minds using the word of God for their benefit, they will preach happiness through the riches men could get and that God wants them to be rich, they will take away repentance, preach into sinning, and away from the suffering through the cross... Instead of deny yourselves, they shall say: "you need to be happy and you have the right to be happy", instead of taking your cross daily they will say: "God doesn't want you to sacrifice anything, our God doesn't want you to suffer", instead of following Jesus they will say: "Follow me"... Money will be the main focus of society and not God, when it was spoken by our Lord that **"You can't serve God and money, you can't have two masters."**

- Longinus: "This is so wicked... it's an abomination!"

- "Men will start a silent war with God in order to erase Him from the hearts of His servants, and many will fall... Some will question the gift of life out the hands of Almighty Father, some will open churches for non-believers, they will say that God shall bless a family of sodomites and the list goes on and on."

- Longinus: "What about the church... will the church survive like this?"

- "The church will survive, but many will suffer greatly... some will infiltrate the church to plant the seeds of iniquity, many will give the Holy Flesh in the hand without the church being under persecution this will lead to an horrible abuse, creating the impression that it is only bread that it's been eaten at the Holy banquet, some will oppose their brothers out of the thirst of power, many will defy obedience and also practice sodomy with some in the church; it'll be difficult time to love Christ and serve Him, but the ones who persevere until the end, shall get all His Mercy."

- Longinus: "I seek forgiveness from my Lord as in my life I once tasted man, I am an abomination... I truly repent of this sin... "

- "My Sweet soldier, you were forgiven of this sin a long time ago, and not only that... you acknowledge that you'd sin and truly repented and decided not doing it again, it's a good thing to make reparations for the sake of getting His Sweet Mercy; now this child, Christ said that if a prostitute truly repents and believe, she shall enter heaven first... well, if a sodomite embrace His Mercy, truly repents and renounce sinning that sodomite shall enter second... it is truly difficult to enter heaven, but His Mercy is the one that creates saints only."

- Longinus: (Crying) I thank you my Sweet Jesus... I thank you for your Mercy."

The angel took me back where I was, I took Aphrodisius and went out to preach, our work was always the same but we did it with joy and happiness, I've always had that pain in my side, my dreams about killing Jesus gave me that pain, at the beginning wasn't that painful, but sometimes it was unbearable; the people always come with the sick and they were healed and converted, demons always came out screaming (that wasn't a shocker), but the ones that always brought me to my knees since I was baptized... (ALWAYS), it was the blind.

Each time somebody come to me with an impaired eyesight, I always remember how I got my sight back, I knew I was forgiven, I knew it was foretold that no bone of His shall be broken, but I just couldn't help it, since so many converted, people from all over Cappadocia came to regained their eyesight, sometimes I had too much pain in my side that I couldn't lift my right arm, I took this suffering out of Love this wasn't a payback or anything like it, I'm a soldier of Christ and He suffers every day for all of us, taking a little bit of His pain is like when the Cyrene man helped Him with the Cross... for me it's an Honor I don't deserve.

It was a week since the angel spoke to me so I assume that Pilate's assassins are almost at the door, at any time it could be my last day on earth. That morning Aphrodisius was preaching until guards from the Governor took him to jail, a little later he was in front of him and he didn't like us destroying most of the idols in the city, then he showed Aphrodisius more idols that were going to be put in the city as the governor was preparing to make everybody worship idols.

- Governor: "You have been found guilty of destroying idols all over Cappadocia... a proper penalty shall be given."

- Aphrodisius: "You are a devil worshiper! devil worshiper! devil worshiper!

- Governor: "Silence... guards!... cut this man's tongue at once! Let's see if he can say those nasty things to me again!"

They cut his tongue in front of a crowd and took him out of the palace and left him there. Some brothers brought him back to me.

- Longinus: "Hello Aphrodisius..."

Immediately the Holy Spirit let him speak without a tongue, and everybody was marveled by God's power...

- Longinus: "Are you ready for a little more my brother Aphrodisius?"

- Aphrodisius: "Yes... all in the name of Jesus our Lord."

That night I was walking throughout the city and some knights came riding their horses and asked...

- "Where we could find someone named Longinus? We heard that he lives here in Caesarea and we have important business with him!"

- Longinus: "My fellow knight, you all look tired... let me show you some courtesy as I was too a soldier a long time ago, I shall tell you afterwards where exactly this Longinus is."

- "You were a soldier huh?... well, fair enough..."

I took them to our house, Aphrodisius which also deserted the military was there, he knew what I was about to do as the Holy Spirit showed him my intentions, Aphrodisius decided to die in martyrdom with me that day. We spoke for long about the military, I served them like I was serving my Lord and Savior Jesus, Aphrodisius did as well, and afterwards they wanted to know our names as they felt identified with us.

- Longinus: "Yes this is Aphrodisius a deserter like me... Longinus."

- "Is this a Joke?"

- Longinus: "No joke my friend, we deserted the military seeking our Lord Jesus and we found him, this warrant for our deaths is our doing since we deserted our troops, please follow your orders."

They pleaded us to flee, they wanted us to escape, but we refused... after a while the commander told us that they needed to report to the Governor first before they could carry out their orders and his last words were:

- "Please leave Longinus; we don't want to kill you."

- Longinus: "Since you have to go to the governor you could go right ahead and do so, tomorrow we shall appear in front of the governor because we need to settle something, and there shall take our heads as ordered, please understand that this our doing for not fulfilling our pledge as soldiers to the armies of Rome, we don't want to owe anybody, so we could face our Lord without owing nothing to no one here on earth."

- "As you wish...tomorrow it is!"

They went away with a sad and long face, but the thing is that once they knew I was in town, they can't go back and say we didn't find him, or he escape, once they go into the governor's palace and show him our death warrants, the governor will acknowledge that we are living in Cappadocia and signed off the orders.

We went to sleep with the a little fear inside of what tomorrow might bring to us, all this thoughts that didn't want to leave my head, and knew these thoughts of doubts weren't mine, so I started to pray to my Lord:

- Longinus: "Please my Sweet Jesus, don't leave me behind, please instead be by my side, remember your soldier, the soldier who loves You! I will do whatever You ask of me, even though I have no merits to gain any graces or favors, all I want is Your Mercy please my Sweet Lord, that's all I'm asking, that's all I want."

Immediately the devil was there telling me that I had no chance to enter heaven...

- "That's right you don't have any merits monk, there's no way that you will enter heaven, you have done more evil than good in this world, but if you surrender to me I shall grant you many riches and I shall revoke your death warrant in an instant!."

- Longinus: "Leave satan in the name of Jesus Christ my Lord, because only the praise and the Glory are for His Father, the Holy Spirit and Him, not even death can stop me from loving Him... be gone."

- "You shall regret this monk when I get you under my control."

- Longinus: "That shall never happen because I'm relying on His Mercy... be gone."

Then he disappeared, after a while the angel of the Lord came to me and gave me a few words to take with me tomorrow.

- "You use faith how it supposed to be used as all this good works happened in your hands, you took the Holy Flesh and Blood knowing that you're not worthy, well done! You let the Lord shape you with the Holy Spirit in order for you to be what He envisioned of you since your creation in heaven, you prayed, fast, suffered patiently, and did what the Lord wanted..."

- Longinus: "Why are you saying all of this to me...? I only wanted to love Him like He loved me... what is going on?"

- "Tomorrow my dear soldier rely on His Mercy alone and trust it, because only His Mercy is the one that will take you to be with Him forever, no man is worthy to be near of such Holiness, but this is why His Blood and Water was pour to the ground, so that all men know that is only through His Mercy that Heaven can be reach... rely on it, breath it, know it, be it and trust in Him. Jesus said Himself: **"The kingdom of heaven is like a treasure buried in a field, which a person finds and hides again, and out of joy goes and sells all that he has and buys that field."** Like Dismas recognized who was beside him in the Cross and asked for His Mercy, you must also do."

- Longinus: "Thank you my brother, thank you for your patience with me, I know I'm a worthless tool, but when this tool is in the hands of Jesus... it works!"

The angel disappeared with a smile on his face and I went to sleep and I had the same dream again, this time it was me versus me, Longinus on the cross and the old me piercing my side with the lance, the pain was horrendous but I didn't die even though I was pierced many times...then, my Lord came down from the heavens and the old me ran away.

- Jesus: "All shall come to the death hill, one by one, either to gain salvation or to have damnation forever, why have a short mortal life full of pleasures of the flesh when you can have an eternity with unimaginable joy, there is no earthly word to describe the things that I have prepared for your happiness in my Father's house."

- Longinus: "I want to be with you Lord forever if you let me, I repent of all of my sins and want your Mercy now and forever, it doesn't matter that I have to live in heaven in a small corner, please Lord... with your Mercy in me, I only need two meters in your presence forever, that's how I want to live, it doesn't matter if I stay in those two meters forever, if I'm in your presence that is good enough for me."

The dream ended and I had no pain in my side like I always did, it was tomorrow and after the prayers me and Aphrodisius went to see the governor, he didn't want to see me there so they took us to some sort of an arena were people were coming in to see our execution, there many people were shouting and cursing us, and very few were crying in silence.

- Governor: "This man and his friend always destroyed our statues and healed the sick with the help of demons; because they deserted their military duties today they will face death!"

I addressed the people with the voice of the Holy Spirit...

- Longinus: "It was the power of the One true God through His only begotten Son Jesus, who was killed in Jerusalem for our sins, our God the Father resurrected Him and Gave Him the Glory and the power and now seats at the right side of Him in heaven!."

- Governor: "These are all lies! We have our own gods and they are more powerful than yours!"

- Longinus: "Now all this idols here in this arena will disappear like sand in the wind and be gone with your wicked tongue!"

- Governor: "What tongue or what teeth? If you shall have no more... Guards!"

Immediately the guards came out and took me by my two hands and they first pulled out my teeth (it was horrendously painful), but all I need is my Lord's Mercy... they were all laughing, then another guard grabbed my mouth, pulled out my tongue and cut it with a knife.

- Governor: "Ha, ha, ha, ha, now... did a cat took out your tongue? What is going on Longinus, you had a big mouth and now it seems that's no more."

- Longinus: "For this you shall be blinded, and the health of your body shall flee, because you didn't recognize that God is the One true God and His Son is the Lord."

All the people there were amazed that I could talk after my tongue got cut, the Governor immediately was blinded and all the idols there started to disappear with the wind, all the people were praising God and His Son Jesus for these miracles.

- Governor: "Please Aphrodisius help me, tell Longinus to pray for me to Jesus in order for me to regain my health back."

- Aphrodisius: "I don't know why you are speaking to me; I shouldn't talk as well, since you also took my tongue out remember?"

- Governor: "Please…please, God is truly the One true God and Jesus is His Son, I truly believe!"

- Longinus: "I will do so if you promise to let Pilate's man pay off our debt with the military cutting our heads now."

- Governor: "But Longinus that is madness…"

- Longinus: "No is not, nobody has to die because of us, this debt has to be paid off today…"

Then the governor gave the order to cut off our heads and with a tear in his eyes the soldier did his duties… The blood that came from my head, sprinkled to the governor and he was immediately cured, his health came back, our comrades immediately took both of our heads and ride to Jerusalem and show Pontius Pilate both of the deserter's heads.

We were both in the dark when our Mother came for us in a radiant cloud…

- Mary: "Hello my children, I've come to take you to heaven as my Son's wishes it so."

- Longinus: "Sweet is the hour when we are together Mother, Sweet is thy Mercy which is showing us your Son, our King and our Savior…"

We started to ascend to the heavens, Aphrodisius was overwhelmed by Love and couldn't say a word, we saw Israel, the Kingdoms, Empire, tribes and other groups of people being left behind, the clouds are gone, so are the moon and the sun; right ahead... a flash of light, warmth and a tender light, one that was embracing us all around and within. We got to a place where everything that you see is a million times beautiful than back home, flowers singing and praising the King of Kings, the greenest grass we have ever seen, we could see and hear better, we saw people rejoicing and loving Almighty Father at the feet of His palace, the Music was everywhere in a melodious tone and at the same time! It wasn't surprising, that the music of others praising all around, were making a big symphony of Love, there was light everywhere, angels flying everywhere, some even announcing our entrance to our divine King Holy tribunal, Aphrodisius went ahead and got judge first as I waited for my turn, I saw a familiar face... Archangel St. Michael.

- Longinus: "Sweet Commander, blessed are my eyes watching you now..."

- St. Michael: "Soldier! We were told you were coming by our Lord... I'm glad that you embraced His Mercy!"

- Longinus: "Me too Commander, I'm glad that I did..."

- St. Michael: "Don't worry much my friend, our Lord gave you His Mercy every day and each time you did embrace it, the suffering was minimal compared to our King's passion, everybody must suffer a little bit from what life give you, in order to come here, but pain and suffering alone won't do it, but His Mercy can... I'm happy for you."

- St. Michael: "Now go... our King is ready for you..."

- Longinus: "Thank you Commander!"

I entered the Holy tribunal; there... the Judge was waiting for this unworthy soul...

- Jesus: "Sweet soldier! I've been waiting for you, It's been long since that day we met on the Golgotha..."

- Longinus: "True my love, I suffered that day all through my life and learned to cherish that day forever, couldn't do it without Your Mercy as it was Your Mercy that took me out of the darkness I had in me."

- Jesus: "This is why you're coming to me with no stains, I forgave you all of your sins each time and you paid with your life the disobedience you did in the army and everything was settled by blood, you followed all the instructions by my disciples...my priests! You fought darkness like you fought when servicing the army of Rome but in the highest levels of obedience, faith and charity... you once told my Mother that you will follow the example of Dismas as He embraced My Mercy nailed to the cross and you did, the persecution started through the Jews and followed with everybody else... you were chosen by my Father from the beginning of your creation to have the opportunity to fulfill the prophecy, by not crushing any of my bones, you gave to the world a sea of My Blood and Water... blessed is he who cover himself with both! Outside of sinning against the Holy Spirit, the hardest headed sinner can be saved through My Mercy, but that can only be achieved by true and sincere repentance and believing that I'm the King of Kings, the Lord and Savior, the Truth, the Light and the Way."

He then raised His hand and touched my face...

- Jesus: "Come my child and enjoy my Father's Love forever, He will be pleased when I present you before Him as from now on your job is to pray to my Father for all the blind in the world to recover their sight and the spiritually blind to open their hearts to my eternal Mercy."

I came out as the angels were singing a welcoming song to the eternal Kingdom of Love, Dismas was waiting outside the tribunal and gave me a smile, some of the people I knew in my mortal life was already there, Cornelius, Stephaton, Mary, my guardian angel (by the way his name is Axel), but didn't saw Aphrodisius...

- Dismas: "Hey sweet soldier..."

- Longinus: "Hey sweet thief..."

- Dismas: "I prayed for you since the day Jesus ascended, which was the day I got judged...here in heaven there are no days or nights... only eternity, we are living in the arms of Love where there's only light forever..."

- Longinus: "Why from the day Jesus ascended?"

-Dismas: "Because Jesus said on that Merciful moment, that we were both going to be in paradise... that day I was taken to paradise along with a few souls, we were in paradise on the other side of the river enjoying God's Might as we waited for His Ascension, He kept His word and fulfilled prophecy by resurrecting on the third day, then He stayed with his disciples a little bit longer, ascended, Judged me, and gave me the job to pray for all thieves and criminals, since most of your life you killed out of boredom, you fell in my territory... so all the praise to I AM for His Son Jesus for giving you the Treasure of the Heavens, which is His Mercy."

- Mary: "If you ask yourself about your brother Aphrodisius, he is in the purgatory cleaning himself from a little bit of stain that he had, he is going to be there for half a day and then he will come out to enjoy God's love forever."

How incredible is God's love? He really has shown great Mercy, nothing is impossible for my Lord for those who truly love Him, Aphrodisius wasn't there yet, but in God's eternal Mercy he has a place for those who has some little stains (benign sins) as nothing can enter paradise with a stain, everybody is Judged in His Holy Tribunal in order to administer his Mighty Justice and Mercy for those who deserve salvation or damnation forever. Jesus our Lord said it: **And whosoever speaketh a word against the Son of man, it shall be forgiven him: but whosoever speaketh against the Holy Ghost, it shall not be forgiven him, neither in this world, <u>neither in the world to come.</u>**"

After you're in paradise no appeals can be given, for the ones with benign little stains the purgatory was made, a rich boy who asked Jesus how to enter the Kingdom of God, instead of following our Lord decided to go back to his riches and the disciples wondered who can be saved after Jesus saying: **"It is easier for a camel to go through the eye of a needle, than for a rich man to enter into the kingdom of God."** Then the Lord of Lords explained to them **"With men it is impossible, but not with God: for with God all things are possible."** People either don't know or don't want to know anything about sainthood in the world today, but again nothing can enter heaven with a stain; Jesus wants YOU for Him as He reveals His Mercy for you, the Treasure is open and bleeds GOLD each day, gold that Dismas appreciated and the humble servant Longinus did, we need to repent every day and follow Him to the Golgotha where we are going to be crucified, if you would like to be like Dismas, repent sincerely of your sins and give yourself to Jesus today by saying with a true heart this with me: I embrace your Love Jesus, I embrace the Son of God, I embrace my cross, I embrace your Kingdom and deny the world now, forgive me Jesus I love you.

It's a war out there, His servant and slave Longinus fought with weapons given out of His Mercy, He won the battle for you already as He died for us in the cross... I hope that you open your heart today... it is my most sincere wish; it is the base of my prayer. Amen

To be a saint...

Requires courage...

Requires a yes...

Requires knowledge...

The knowledge that on your own, you can't be a saint...

You need to want it...

You need to ask it...

You need to achieve it...

For the need of your brothers, you have to be a saint...

You can't be a saint without humility...

You can't be a saint without sacrifice...

You can only be a saint with Jesus Mercy...

Do know, you can't enter heaven without being a Saint.

Prayer to the tool of Mercy of the Lord...

Oh! **Mary** conceived without sin, pray to your Son our Lord Jesus Christ...

To please turn the waters of our lives into another color,

change my Lord Jesus Christ, like in Cana...

The waters of our lives into wine, so our lives change to another color...

The color of Your Love. Amen.

BOOK III:

DIAMONDS

PREFACE

Little gems came from His Almighty Hand and big Diamonds He wants back, nothing with a stain shall enter His presence, so a Saint you need to become, there are many saints in the Church and even more that we don't know about, because some saints shall make miracles happen only through a yes from the Lord... When someone around the world dies because of the good news of the Gospel, Life they shall find in Jesus, some diamonds will be small, medium, or big (saints)... but through His blood and water some rough edges will be polished, stony hearts will be replaced with natural hearts, some shall find that some things are true whether you believe in them or not, as their rough edges will need a little time through the Holy flames to get done. Many wolves are leading the sheep right know to lead them stray so they may never become a diamond... Jesus Mercy is the only thing we need to rely and trust, His Mercy can be eaten and worshiped every day in the Holy Banquet and Holy Sacrament. Let's pray for workers to lead us to sainthood, workers that thirst for souls for Jesus. Amen.

I

What is a diamond? A precious stone consisting of a crystalline form of pure carbon. Heat and pressure over time needs to occur in order to get a diamond from natural coal, at the molecular level, the coal changes so it could become a diamond, no other stone is more important within history than a diamond. Men had fight for centuries to get such a precious thing in their hands, blood have been spilled over such vane desire. The worth of a diamond is driven by the demand and the worth depends on it's purity, shape, size and weight (carats)... Some diamonds could become priceless depending on their carats, rarity and cut, for example the Kooh-I-Noor currently in the grasps of the British Crown and also a pale yellow diamond with the French Crown collection at display within the Louvre are priceless, these diamonds, the Cullinan, the Hope, De Beers Centenary, the Steinmetz Pink and many more are all beautiful, but no even all the diamonds in the world are more precious than the 0.0000000001% of a small fraction of our souls. I was with my wife when God gave me the grace to see such a wonderful spectacle, a miracle out of His Mercy.

It was one of those days when my wife wanted to go shopping, we went to one of her favorite places: Ross... to tell you the truth and I guess for most average man, going shopping with the wife is a torture, but is one thing that we must do for the good health of a relationship between a couple; anyways, my wife was checking dresses out, I was thinking about God and how sweet He is, all of the sudden in my mind came the thought: "If I could see You Lord in every person it'll be awesome" and before I could even finish that sentence in my mind, the Lord grant me the grace to see how people were reflecting His Love, the flesh wasn't a problem for all His Might, all these people in front of me were SHINNING like diamonds! I was so amaze by His Mercy for letting me see this great miracle of love, I was told in my mind that actually they were shining not because of their own strength but in reality they were reflecting God *"one whose appearance sparkled like jasper and carnelian. Around the throne was a halo as brilliant as an emerald."* **(Rev 4:3)**, God is everywhere and everybody were doing their own things at this store, their souls were like mirrors of God's beauty all around us, they were shinning gracefully...

The light reflected was a reminder that His Mercy is everywhere thanks to the sufferings of His only begotten Son, Jesuschrist. Blood and water came from His side to transform the whole world, all where shinning except one person that came across me during these incredible and beautiful miracle, this young female with exercise or sports attire, where as you could imagine everything that she wore was short, so short that her attires could reflect only indecency (in some countries that young female could get either in jail or worse.) But nothing my dear ones... it's the way of the world; the whole vision stopped with that lack of decency between her and my eyes, yes my eyes crying out for more indecency! That's how the flesh works and the flesh is weak for some of the pleasures the devil is allowed to throw your way, our culture is love thyself and that culture conflicts with the Kingdom of God which calls to deny thyself. Anyways, the young female went in another direction and thank you Jesus the vision came again, the reflection of such beautiful light came to me and it gave me enormous sense of peace, I wish that anybody during their lifetime sees what I saw that afternoon, such a beautiful light reflected in all men, women and child.

That vision didn't came to me like that afternoon again, I was seeing people shinning for maybe 20-30 minutes at the store and I've prayed for it to come back, the effect of that awesome vision it was so calming and peaceful, the thing is that when you experience God you never want that experience to end, once I was entering Weshore plaza through Sears store in Tampa, we were coming out to go to Payless shoe source and across the hall I saw this African American lady, between 60 to 70 years old and she was shining most than anybody I've seen so far, I was delighted that God gave me the grace again to see His Mercy again, she was with her whole family I presume and because I didn't want to alarm her about this vision given to me I didn't approach her... she must Love Jesus more than anything in life, more than life itself !! Oh God how sweet is your Mercy, there are those who loves Jesus and those who reflect His Mercy, but the ones that will truly enjoy that Mercy is whoever embraces Him like the Son of God, the Savior, the only Truth the Light and the Way, the One who died for us in the Cross... so they could become true clean gems in the eyes of the Lord and enjoy heaven. Amen.

II

Our Father Almighty has plan with no errors and all starts and ends with His love, from the beginning God had His only begotten Son in line for sacrifice to conquer death and give men hope for eternity, because the law required that all who sinned must die **(Rom 6:23)**, but on top of the law a bridge was given, a bridge of Mercy through the passion, cross and resurrection of Jesuschrist, for those who believe in Jesus they will be truly freed to achieve eternity. God needed His only begotten Son to be born in the world in the most clean recipient, so God created something so beautiful, so magnificent and clean to carry the most Holy inside, the arch of the new covenant and the most pure diamond of them all *"Then God's temple in heaven was opened, and the ark of his covenant could be seen in the temple. There were flashes of lightning, rumblings, and peals of thunder, an earthquake, and a violent hailstorm."* **(Rev 11:19)**, the new Eve to cleanse the name of women everywhere from old Eve's deeds and show humanity the Motherly Love of God: Mary.

Most people misunderstands the role of Mary in the history of salvation but we could summarize Her role in the following comparison: The sun is the center of the solar system no other star is the center and there is no other huge source of light other than the sun, you could see nebulas, chaos and destruction out there but all source of light astrologically speaking comes from a star, the subsequent light is reflected in everything else... God is that sun and source of light everywhere, natural and beautiful light everywhere. Creation first began by Light and anything else was seen in the light, God saw that it was good and also everything that followed, everything was good in the eyes of God for the upcoming great creation: man and women. Light had it's time during the day and the sun shine while some other places were kept in dark, but God is so Merciful that He created the Moon and the stars beyond so that men could marveled in God's Might, the moon and the far distant stars were there for us every night.

The Moon rolls around earth giving inspiration to many poets, for people to dream in reaching her and wondered around her beauty, the moon reflects the rays of the sun so that His children could see a little better at night, it's tough to wonder around when a new moon is out there, shutting down most of the light that reflects upon her surface but that doesn't mean that the moon isn't there... You see, the moon doesn't have any power of her own, if the moon could say anything right now, you would never hear her saying something like: "Let me shine with my own power!"

The Moon is nothing but a tool of the Sun, the light is reflected in her surface for the sake of mankind, and again, the moon doesn't have any power at all, only the power given by the sun.

Mary the Mother of our Lord Jesus is like the moon, she doesn't have any power of her own but only the power given to Her by Father Almighty: His only Son, and that is Her power, what she has is... Mercy and what is Her Mercy? The Blessed fruit of thy womb Jesus, that's it... whoever thinks that Mary could save a person on Her own account will find nothing but their doom, but the ones that cries out to Her so that Her Son gives them His Mercy that's how they find life through Her hands.

Jesus gave His own Mother to us at the cross to all humanity and it is really a need for anybody that is ordained in any position inside the Church to rely on this powerful tool of Mercy given by Jesus, He said: "Son, behold your Mother... Mother, behold your son." **(John 19:26-27)**. That same day the disciple took Mary in his house, why John was so beloved? because not only he was a disciple and a friend, out of the apostles he was the only one that could take care of Mary with the same love as Jesus always did here on earth. John was reclined in Jesus chest and John alone at that time heard the most beautiful sound that any human ever has heard before, he heard the heart of Jesus and the mystery of His Mercy overflowing for all mankind, the only one who knew that sound before John: Mary herself... John was at the cross but who was John? He was a not only a disciple, apostle, a friend, but a priest!! Yes a priest that took Mary the Mother of Jesus our savior into his home, and what is the house of John?

The house of a priest is the Church and no priest can go on into their daily tasks without being in front of the cross to receive Jesus Mother into their lives, they will not be very efficient priests, there hasn't being a saint yet that hasn't love Mary.

Mary never doubted the Father's word, She said yes to all of His commands, She never sinned and assisted Almighty Father's Son with Her love and Her silence; She will never ask anything outside of God's plan and His Holy word, many people has fallen in the deceit to say bad things about Her, many people has fallen in the deceit to ignore Her, others has fallen in the deceit to adore Her, but all this bad behavior/omission/adoration for Her, only works negatively towards that person, adoration towards Her only gives Her repugnance. Mary only wants for all men to be saved through her Son, not Her... So it's alright to pray to Her for Mercy? Of course is more than alright, Mary will seek the favor of Her Son Jesus. **(Psalm 45)**.

"My heart is stirred by a noble theme, as I sing my ode to the king. My tongue is the pen of a nimble scribe.
You are the most handsome of men; fair speech has graced your lips, for God has blessed you forever.
Gird your sword upon your hip, mighty warrior! In splendor and majesty ride on triumphant!
In the cause of truth and justice may your right hand show you wondrous deeds.
Your arrows are sharp; peoples will cower at your feet; the king's enemies will lose heart.
Your throne, O god, stands forever; your royal scepter is a scepter for justice.
You love justice and hate wrongdoing; therefore God, your God, has anointed you with the oil of gladness above your fellow kings.
With myrrh, aloes, and cassia your robes are fragrant. From ivory-paneled palaces stringed instruments bring you joy
Daughters of kings are your lovely wives; a princess arrayed in Ophir's gold comes to stand at your right hand.
Listen, my daughter, and understand; pay me careful heed. Forget your people and your father's house,
that the king might desire your beauty. He is your lord; honor him, daughter of Tyre. Then the richest of the people will seek your favor with gifts.
All glorious is the king's daughter as she enters, her raiment threaded with gold;

*In embroidered apparel she is led to the king. The maids of her train
are presented to the king.
They are led in with glad and joyous acclaim; they enter the palace of
the king.
The throne of your fathers your sons will have; you shall make them
princes through all the land.
I will make your name renowned through all generations; thus nations
shall praise you forever."*

The wine ran short in Cana and She noticed *"On the third day
there was a wedding in Cana in Galilee, and the mother of Jesus was
there. Jesus and his disciples were also invited to the wedding. When
the wine ran short, the mother of Jesus said to him, "They have no
wine." Jesus said to her, "Woman, how does your concern affect me?
My hour has not yet come." His mother said to the servers, "Do
whatever he tells you." Now there were six stone water jars there for
Jewish ceremonial washings, each holding twenty to thirty gallons.
Jesus told them, "Fill the jars with water." So they filled them to the
brim. Then he told them, "Draw some out now and take it to the
headwaiter." So they took it. And when the headwaiter tasted the
water that had become wine, without knowing where it came from,
the headwaiter called the bridegroom and said to him, "Everyone
serves good wine first, and then when people have drunk freely, an
inferior one; but you have kept the good wine until now." Jesus did
this as the beginning of his signs in Cana in Galilee and so revealed his
glory, and his disciples began to believe in him."* **(John 2:1-11)**, She
went to Her Son and Jesus performed His first Miracle, She
doesn't have any power of Her own but the one given by Almighty
Father Himself: Mercy incarnated... the Blessed fruit of thy womb
Jesus, the One that could save us if we embrace Him truly, the
Mother of God the Son, tireless shall seek favors from Jesus for
those who truly Honors Him. Amen.

III

In order to have a Diamond you need coal, as black as night you could find coal today anywhere, there is so much coal in the world but there's a lack in diamonds everywhere, the price is driven by the lack of diamonds but also it's rarity.

There's some diamonds out there but not as rare as Father Pio, Francis of Assisi, Maria Goretti, Gemma Galgani, Faustina Kowalska, Therese of Lisieux, Rita of Cascia; there are lots of diamonds out there big and small, most of them are in the hands of God in heaven and others walking the earth as we speak, spreading the good news of Jesuschrist.

Going back to coal, this is exactly what we have every day on earth: souls as black as night, some light black, some black and some blacker than the holes you find in space *"but if your eye is bad, your whole body will be in darkness. And if the light in you is darkness, how great will the darkness be."* **(Matt 6:23)**; every human in this world gets a stain called original sin and with a hardheaded decision all throughout life we put more darkness into our souls, sin doesn't taste bad... it taste awesomely good, if the taste of sin to our flesh was a bad one... nobody would do it, if we knew what we are putting into our souls, if we could see how that stain looks... we wouldn't do it, the stench comes from the father of all lies and if we could smell that we would puke all day... but we can't see or smell this in spiritual proportions like some saints did, but do know this: **ALL SIN (OUTSIDE OF THE BLASPHEMY TOWARDS THE HOLY SPIRIT), CAN BE ERASED THROUGH JESUS MERCY TODAY!**

The Mercy of our Lord and Savior can erase the most insane and wicked sins out there, for those that have many sins... Jesus can erase them, for those who have a conscience with no rest; Jesus will put them to rest... Jesus our Lord is that heat and pressure over time that coal needs to become a diamond and He could turn you into an awesome saint as nothing can enter heaven with a stain *"but nothing unclean will enter it, nor any (one) who does abominable things or tells lies. Only those will enter whose names are written in the Lamb's book of life."* **(Rev 21:27)**.

This is why Jesus tells us after we convert to Him: *"Whoever wishes to come after me must deny himself, take up his cross, and follow me."* **(Matt 16:24)** Practically He is warning us that in order to gain heaven we need to suffer a little bit *"Resist him, steadfast in faith, knowing that your fellow believers throughout the world undergo the same sufferings. The God of all grace who called you to his eternal glory through Christ (Jesus) will himself restore, confirm, strengthen, and establish you after you have suffered a little."* **(1Peter 5:9-10)**.

Jesus himself is telling all of us that we need to deny ourselves, which only means that we need to deny that sinful way of life that the world likes to see from us and also deny our flesh certain pleasures, Jesus says that we need to take our cross daily and this is where the suffering comes, the daily things that hurt us we need to place them in Jesus hands and suffer them in His Name... suffering will shape our hearts into a more mature and holier Christians *"Not only that, but we even boast of our afflictions, knowing that affliction produces endurance, and endurance, proven character, and proven character, hope, and hope does not disappoint, because the love of God has been poured out into our hearts through the holy Spirit that has been given to us."* **(Rom 5:3-5)**.

There are no situations where the Sweet Mercy of our Lord can't erase: prostitution, sodomy, addiction, lesbianism, pornography, theft, murder, bestiality, adultery, blasphemies from the clergy, and much, much more... we all need to embrace His Mercy now and forever by faith, deny ourselves and follow Him, nobody says is not a difficult path because it is *"How narrow the gate and constricted the road that leads to life. And those who find it are few."* **(Matt 7:14)**, nobody says that the cross is not heavy because: life is hard... but as you walk the path the cross becomes a little light because Jesus already took the guilt of all upon Himself, Jesus wants to encourage all who love Him to take the cross as He says: *"Take my yoke upon you and learn from me, for I am meek and humble of heart; and you will find rest for your selves. For my yoke is easy, and my burden light."* **(Matt 11:29-30)**.

Jesus will go in front of you as you follow Him, He will lead you to the Golgotha where you either follow the example of Dysmas the good thief or Gestas the bad thief, you will either embrace the King of Mercy for your salvation or deny Him for your damnation; hopefully you will embrace His Mercy so He could say to you: *"Amen, I say to you, today you will be with me in Paradise."* **(Luke 23:43)**. Jesus says that a prostitute that repents shall enter the Kingdom of God first *"Which of the two did his father's will?" They answered, "The first." Jesus said to them, "Amen, I say to you, tax collectors and prostitutes are entering the kingdom of God before you."* **(Matt 21:31)**, a thief (Dysmas) entered heaven with Him after he died on the cross with Jesus.

His Mercy is for ALL SINNERS who seek salvation, no matter the condition of their souls if you truly repent and cry out to His Mercy you shall get it... The Treasure of the Heavens, the Mercy of our Lord Jesus, the ones who cannot be saved are the ones who destroys the Temple of the Holy Spirit (by suicide) or by their own lips by blaspheming the Holy Spirit *"Therefore, I say to you, every sin and blasphemy will be forgiven people, but blasphemy against the Spirit will not be forgiven."* **(Matt 12:31)**.

Some will have a cross bigger than others, some will have to sacrifice much in order to reach heaven, the path is led by Christ, who sees your sacrifice, who sees your denial to the world and your flesh, who sees your joy for the heavenly things, who will give His gold from His Holy side and through that same opening blood and water will pour unto you, you who embraced Him dearly and with that much Mercy you shall have eternity by becoming a Saint.

Becoming a Saint only requires a yes on your part, requires sacrifice, love and humility and again this can be achieve by embracing Christ, embracing His Mercy, Obeying him as you follow Him to the death Hill throughout life carrying your daily cross, this little suffering will shape your faith, graces shall come to you... Hope, Humility, Obedience, Charity and many more just give your life to Him without questions, repent each day, deny yourself, carry your big cross and follow Him to eternity.

IV

This is something very special to me, something that I was struggling to write about, one moment of pure Tenderness from great Love, sometimes we pray and many times we ask our Lord to give us the usual: health, obstacles we need to overcome, love, sometimes strength, and most of the times we pray for our love ones... but once in a while for those in the path, there comes a time that you ask the Lord something strange and beautiful, a grace maybe, a miracle perhaps, something that makes you think for a while, something that you know it wasn't you, that you're not intelligent enough to make that petition, something that came from within, something from the very depths of Love itself...

From the Holy Spirit. As I write this words at 6:23 a.m. in the morning at the very end of my shift that rolls all through the night, my heart is literally on fire *"Then they said to each other, "Were not our hearts burning within us while he spoke to us on the way and opened the scriptures to us?"* **(Luke 24:32)** and I have to say that it's a fire so beautiful that I wish that all of you burn with it, right know this fire tells me that it's ok to share this little secret of intimacy and love of mine, this secret that I wanted to hide from the world and cherish forever, because of me being afraid of giving away all my intimate moments with God... but in the end I'll do what He wants because I love Him.

I was praying one day and out of the blue I asked my Lord Jesus to take me back to my first Love, and when those words came out of my mouth, immediately I knew it was a beautiful idea, because my first Love and your first Love (even if you don't know it yet), is Almighty Father in heaven.

One time at my Job I had a colleague we were talking about God, and we were debating something that frankly I don't remember what it was, but she end up asking me if I wanted to die... I said: "Yes." She was shocked, but I explained to her as I also once explained to my wife that I have a problem with Christians that want to go to heaven but don't want to die, I explained to my colleague and my wife at home, that I wasn't a fool, I don't want to kill myself or enhance the chances of me getting killed... I love my life, love my wife, my children and of course I'll love to see them grow and experience the greatest gift from God... life. I think it was St. Therese of Lissieux if I'm not mistaken, that once said: "I'm dying because I'm not dying."

The Love of our Lord is unimaginable to compute with the 10% that we use of our brains, and it'll take an eternity to know the Father, what I'm saying is that between my life now (again, which I love), and a life with Jesus in heaven... I choose heaven!

Here's what happened, I started to pray to my Lord about taking me to my first Love for a little more than a week, and it happened... I don't know if I had a vision, I don't know if I was dreaming, everything took place in the Light... I was seeing me... I knew I was recently created, I was resting in the huge hands of Father Almighty, I could see myself in His hands even though that what He had in His hands was different than my physical body... what He had was my soul, then a tender warmth came from His smile and that warmth gave me life... I lifted my head as I woke up and saw Jesus smiling at me... right beside Jesus the Holy Spirit was also seeing me... they were smiling as God the Father Almighty was happy and satisfied to show His creation.

Beautiful Father Almighty was happy to show me to His Son and the Holy Spirit, I tried to lift my head a little bit more and I'm seeing my Lord Jesus and the Holy Spirit, I tried to see the Father but couldn't see His face as it radiated so much Light that I couldn't see a face...

Imagine a room where there is only light beyond any light you have ever seen, but the face of Almighty Father had a Light much, much brighter than the one inside the room... the eyes of my soul couldn't see Him. That is my secret, which gave me so much peace when it happened, every day that I remember that dream or vision, immediately my whole body remembers that nice feeling given through His smile... the warmth that gave me life. I wish you my dear brother that you have that same or better vision of Love as I did, I came to the world to love God only and every day the path gets more difficult as it gets clearer through our Lord Jesus.

Father Almighty sent His only begotten Son in order that we could get salvation, He and His Son knew the violence to be suffered between the mount of olives and the cross, as His beloved creation treated His Son Jesus the way we all did, He knew it would happen like that because He is God... but also He did suffered with His Son as it was necessary *"The Father and I are one."* **(John 10:30)**.

Some things are true whether you believe in them or not and Jesus **IS** the Son of God, and He wants to share eternity with us, that's why He died on the cross for humanity, to freed us from the bondage of sin and death, the vicious cycle was broken and now we can all return home through Jesus Mercy; I saw myself as a little soul in Father Almighty's hands, a little incorrupt soul as I was being prepared to come to the world, a little gem that instead of remaining a gem I got myself into wickedness, malice and sin...

By the time I gave myself to Jesus I was that coal being shaped by His love *"Yet, O LORD, you are our father; we are the clay and you the potter: we are all the work of your hands"* **(Is 64:8)** so much sin and error from my part that He gladly washed away, I came as a little gem from our Father's hands up in heaven and I must grow and become a diamond through my Lord Jesus sweet Mercy. I'm not a saint... but I want to be one, if any of my friends could tell you right now who I am, they will tell you that I'm a difficult person, so I'm not a saint...

If my journey to sainthood was to walk 3 times around the world on foot, all I can tell you is that I have only walk a few centimeters, but I'm with Jesus and I want to become a saint, a diamond of His Mercy.

Why I'm a sharing this? You need to understand for once and for all, this is not our home, we need to return to our real home in heaven, we must believe in Jesus to be truly freed and thrive in His Mercy, Jesus died in the cross as even scientists have proven that Jesus indeed was crucified and murdered (For those who say that he didn't die.), historians from that era has shown He was crucified (Flavius Josephus), whoever denies this is because they like the world and don't care about going to hell; Jesus is the Savior, the Messiah, the Truth, the Light and the Way and only through Him we could go to the Father. **(John 14:6)**.

I'll pray for perseverance for all of us through His Mercy, I'll ask Mother Mary for a miracle of Mercy through Her Son, I'll pray for protection for all who Love Christ, and I'll pray for **YOU** to pray for Mercy today...

If you already have Jesus, look for His Mercy more and more every day, and look always for the Heavenly things, do sacrifice, penitence, daily repentance of you sins, have joy, charity, humility and seek to become a saint... it only requires a yes from you and His sweet, sweet Mercy, I love you brother in Christ and Christ loves you and He wishes you only the best, which is the contents of the Treasure... His Mercy. Amen.

V

Father Grunner has been fighting the good fight, by telling the whole world the truth... the consecration of Russia hasn't been made as our Lady asked to the 3 little kids in Fatima, Portugal; the errors of Russia **DID** travel throughout the world, how many have suffered? Throughout many countries were this ideologies are nothing but a tool of the devil, is it too late to consecrate Russia? Yes indeed the hour is late, but nevertheless is never too late to obey our Lady and consecrate Russia. *"What is your opinion? A man had two sons. He came to the first and said, 'Son, go out and work in the vineyard today.' He said in reply, 'I will not,' but afterwards he changed his mind and went. The man came to the other son and gave the same order. He said in reply, 'Yes, sir,' but did not go. Which of the two did his father's will?" They answered, "The first." Jesus said to them, "Amen, I say to you, tax collectors and prostitutes are entering the kingdom of God before you."* **(Matt 21:28-31)**.

So many had the truth in their hands and were persecuted inside and outside of the Church, St. Francis of Assisi had persecution from the bishop of Assisi but that led to even better things as he got recognition from the pope, Father Pio was ordered to stay in his cell by the church for some time but he offered his suffering to God, John of the cross was imprisoned by his own brothers of his religious order, he had to escape them and many saints more.

And this is the truth: the Church is Holy by Jesus and the part of the church that is sinful is because of men... so have joy father Grunner, don't be afraid and don't give up.

"Therefore do not be afraid of them. Nothing is concealed that will not be revealed, nor secret that will not be known. What I say to you in the darkness, speak in the light; what you hear whispered, proclaim on the housetops." **(Matt 10:26-27)**.

Nobody wants to remember what past popes have said about communion in the tongue, since most of them before Vatican II favored communion on the tongue and funny thing, this evil appeared after Vatican II and is directly related to the apparitions by our Lady in Quito and Fatima.

Pope Leo the Great (to mention one of many), have spoken in favor about communion in the tongue. Today it is the norm by the Vatican to give communion in the mouth, but in 1977 a permission was given to the bishops of the USA in order to give communion in the hand to avoid danger to the "fragile" believes of some. In the beginning, the church had communion in the hand because the whole church was under persecution.

The Holy Banquet provided by Jesus Himself it is believe by many to happen by communion in the mouth instead of the hand, why? Because within Jew tradition of that era the one leading the banquet needed to put the first piece of food in the mouths of the people attending, also we have details of this as our Lord needed to teach a lesson of brotherly love as He wash the disciples feet *"Then he poured water into a basin and began to wash the disciples' feet and dry them with the towel around his waist."* **(John 13:5)**, but the most important and revealing detail of it was when Jesus dip the morsel and gave it to Judas *"Jesus answered, "It is the one to whom I hand the morsel after I have dipped it." So he dipped the morsel and took it and handed it to Judas, son of Simon the Iscariot."* **(John 13:26)**, first you don't give no one a piece of food already dipped into someone's hands it's a mess, and second the definition of morsel is a small piece of food, a MOUTHFUL... St. Bilas (330-379) said that Holy communion can be only be given in the hand under persecution only, funny thing is that the church was under open persecution until Emperor Constantine made Christianity the religion of the Roman empire, so yes at the beginning communion was in the hand alright, but for those who still advocates against communion in the tongue I got to tell you this...

Once I was having a debate with priest whom I love dearly, I told him that if he could find ANY saint who had received the Eucharist miraculously either by an angel, a saint or Jesus Himself in the hand then I would start taking communion in the hand myself, he then went into the defensive telling me that he needed the ministers of the Eucharist in order to handle communion to the laity...

Of course because all this ministers touch the most Holy body with their unworthy hands, when only priests have that luxury with their consecrated hands as St. Francis once said. *"The kindly man will be blessed, for he gives of his sustenance to the poor. Expel the arrogant man and discord goes out; strife and insult cease. The LORD loves the pure of heart; the man of winning speech has the king for his friend."* **(Prov 22:9-11)**.

Anyways my priest friend knew that the debate ended right there, because **NO SAINT IN THE HISTORY OF THE CHURCH HAS EVER RECEIVE COMMUNION IN THE HAND GIVEN BY AN ANGEL, A SAINT OR JESUS HIMSELF**, not one!

Our souls gain more by recognizing that we are not worthy to take it in the hand, ask yourself: what is more spiritual tongue or the hand? No saint has ever received the Eucharist in the hand by either an angel, a saint or Jesus himself, think about it. Some will contradict me trying to say that I don't know what I'm talking about, that I don't have the necessary studies to say this… That's true but I have the Holy Spirit. I could tell you right now with certainty that I'm a fool, unworthy, and no good person, this is why I try to give my all to Jesus, this why I follow Him because I'm a machine of wickedness and I want my salvation, this is why I accepted Jesus and the gift of the Holy Spirit was given, this is how I know **communion in the hands it's a SIN**, it has become a sin because of all the abuse… we want to be CRUCIFIED WITH HIM not CRUCIFY HIM AGAIN as romans, there is no open and direct persecution to our Church. There has been a great abuse created through this permission given by our dear Church and even though they know it, our bishops don't want to stop it.

(1 Cor 11 27-29):

"Therefore whoever eats the bread or drinks the cup of the Lord unworthily will have to answer for the body and blood of the Lord.
A person should examine himself, and so eat the bread and drink the cup.
For anyone who eats and drinks without discerning the body, eats and drinks judgment on himself."

Should I stay away from the Catholic Church knowing that so many wolves are clothed as sheep? OF COURSE NOT! Because of the few diamonds today walking the earth in the first Church created, these diamonds are those who actually follow Jesus precepts to the letter and at the same time they OBEY, they obey the church like Jesus did obey the Father Almighty up in heaven, they know this facts already written in this pages and they don't walk away from the Church, they stay and walk with Jesus to the Golgotha with their crosses in their backs, what we need to do now more harder than ever it's to PRAY, pray for those who lead, for those who administer, for those who sacrifice everything for our spiritual gain, pray for those who kill us, pray for those who oppose us, pray for all the churches around the world who love Christ, we need to pray today more than ever, so that the owner of the vineyard send more workers, workers that want to be diamonds or better said... who wants to become saints, workers who want to gain souls for Him, workers who are thirsty of His love, thirsty of His Sweet Mercy now, until Kingdom come. Amen.

In the year 2011 the OSCE (Organization for Security and Cooperation in Europe) revealed to the world that every 5 minutes a Christian is killed by their believes, that's 105,000 a year (http://www.catholicculture.org/news/headlines/index.cfm?storyid= 10555), don't be surprise if that number is a little bit more higher than that because of some statistics in places that are difficult to get, places that we don't know how the Church is doing, like North Korea and some other countries where the Church is underground... Blessed are those who die with the beautiful name of our Lord in their mouths, and remember... Many miracles are out there, but none of them saves like the miracle of Jesus in the most Holy Sacrament. Amen.

FINAL WORDS

From the Treasure of Heavens and the writer's life and beliefs...

First my testimony: Before the graduation occurred I was practicing pediatrics in the University's Hospital, I developed a severe bilateral pneumonia (breathing only through breathing devices), then a septicemia, my immunologic natural defenses were not working because of a bone marrow aplasia caused by medications to reduce fever (the medication is called neomelubrina), under these conditions the doctors said that it would take a miracle to save me; many people prayed in many places in the world, **two different people saw Jesus watching me in my bed while in a coma** (7 days) ... after Jesus saved me from certain death, I had to go to New York to repair my trachea through surgery (over 15 surgeries), I had a trachea stenosis caused by the artificial ventilator (breathing machine). After 3 years battling I finally recovered, but a permanent stoma was all that was left from all those surgeries making it difficult for him to go back to medicine again (the stoma was an open window for infections). Jesus appeared to me in a dream and told me that He needed me to speak to all about His Mercy and as proof of this, NO light was going to be the next day, the next day there was no light!! The sky was dark all the gray thick clouds covered up above, the whole day was dark (This happened in New York, I was there at the time), my father who was in Boston called me and I asked him about the conditions of the sky there, not knowing what was going on he replied saying "that it was all dark", then my wife called from Santo Domingo (Dominican Republic), and the same question was asked and she said "the sky was black and with much lightning", after that... I knew what I needed to do, I needed to tell everybody about Jesus Mercy, and what is His Mercy exactly?.

Through this story of Dismas it is revealed as simply Love acting in our behalf, in other words the action of Divine Love. Almighty Father acted by **giving** us Jesus His only Son, to be saved... Jesus had to **die and be resurrected**, and He says in his word that **no one takes** His life **He gives** his life. The Treasure of Heaven is Jesus Mercy and Mercy is Love in action, He acted to save us... He **had to come from Heaven as a poor man** despite owning tons of glory, **suffering, by being scourged, spat upon, getting punched, humiliated and disfigured,** seeing some of the people He shared His life with betraying Him, seeing your own people giving You their back, dying on the cross for all humanity even for the most hard headed sinner and all this out of Love, by definition Mercy is an act of Love from the offended to the aggressor. There are things in life that are true even if you believe in them or not, and Jesus Mercy is one that is real... Jesus Mercy shows the Love of the Father and the Holy Spirit in perfect unity for the salvation of **YOU!** Mercy is for everyone despite sins, look at Peter who betrayed Jesus, look at Paul who was a mass murderer, and look at Dismas who was a thief... pray to get Mercy today! I will pray that you do, may Jesus Mercy shines upon you, may Jesus shows you His beautiful face and lead you to His Father Almighty. Amen

*Jesus told me: "tell the whole world about My Mercy", the story about Dismas the patron saint of thieves for their conversion and Longinus the patron saint for the blind is one of Great Mercy, that's why I got this stories deep in my heart, the true history of the "sweet thief and the sweet soldier" it is not written yet in any book of history, we only know a little bit by holy scripture, I used parables from Holy scripture and all around the Mercy of God through Jesus our Lord and Savior, I also used some legends around them and inspiration from His Mercy, to filled the blank spaces in their biographies and give you a taste of Jesus Mercy. We all know that Dismas and Longinus are in heaven and I hope that all of us imitate them by recognizing that Jesus is the Son of God, the King of Kings and the Lord of lords and be willing to go to the death hill with Him and ask for His Mercy.

*While I was praying the Rosary at work (though I was told not to pray on the job anymore), I was contemplating the sorrowful mysteries, when I was at the Crown of Thorns I asked myself internally: "Jesus suffered from the beginning of the Passion to the end for the sins of mankind from that moment on to the future... for whom exactly He was suffering in the Crown of Thorns?" For my surprise and Joy, Jesus said to me clearly and I'm not schizophrenic: **"Rafael, the Thorns I suffered because of all who say that Love me but doesn't love thy brother."** In that same moment he showed me in a flash, all the times that I had the opportunity to love my brother or sister even if it was a little opportunity and I chose not by not practicing charity. This is why a faith without good works is a dead faith; good works is evidence of Mercy working within... **so be Merciful** like Jesus and His Father were to Dismas and Longinus.

*Mercy can be eaten so listen carefully...Disciple Paul said from the Holy Spirit: "Therefore whoever eats the bread or drinks the cup of the Lord **unworthily will have to answer for the body and blood of the Lord**.1 Cor 11:27.
You'll say "well the Disciples took the bread of life in the hand", nope...sorry, first the disciples were priests and second it is accustomed to give food in your guests mouth in Hebrew tradition, by Jesus time this was the way, you could tell by how Jesus gave a morsel dipped to Judas, how is it that you'll give something dipped to somebody in the hand? It'll be a mess, you could say "well in the hand was how the church used to do back then"... Yes only until emperor Constantine put Christianity as religion, because before Constantine the **whole church was persecuted and this is the only way it should be given by hand, in persecution;** but the sun is setting in the western world... By having the Eucharist in the hand MANY are abusing the Holy Sacrament and this is the danger, right now there's **no active persecution** to the majority of the laity... no reverence of the sacrament, and the sacrament could be treated like it is by many today... like a piece of bread; let's give Christ a chance, let's love Him in the Holy sacrament, let's take Him in the mouth knowing that we are not worthy to take Him in the hand.

*Finally let's **ASK** for **Jesus Mercy** through prayer and communion with a constrict Heart, thirsty to forgive and be forgiven knowing that if you ask you shall receive. "Ask and it will be given to you; seek and you will find; knock and the door will be opened to you." Matthew 7:7. **BE Jesus Mercy** by being an example for others always seeking humility. "Take my yoke upon you and learn from me, for I am meek and humble of heart; and you will find rest for your selves." Matthew 11:29. **GIVE Jesus Mercy** by practicing charity, again a dead faith is the one with NO good works. May Jesus Mercy come upon yourselves, may you be an advocate of Christ, and may he show His Beautiful face to you. Amen.

BIOGRAPHY

I was born in New York the 21st of November 1972, son of Dr. Rafael Gonzalez and Amaury Frias. After my parents got divorced my mother took us to Dominican Republic, so I was raised in Santo Domingo, Dominican Republic; I found Jesus Christ in September 18, 1992 "All of my life never knew that Jesus was alive and I found Him in the Catholic Church." Started a family with Maria Tejada in 1997 my lovely wife, that same year I took medicine as a career at the Universidad Central del Este (UCE) in San Pedro de Macoris and graduating in 2005, right before graduation I got sick, the severity of my illnesses I couldn't practice as a doctor due to the imminent danger of infections through my stoma (see final words to read his testimony), today I'm practicing my faith... advocating Jesus Mercy through the sweetness of receiving the Eucharist in the tongue instead of the hand, I'm currently working at Stetson University in the Public safety department in Saint Petersburg in Florida and hopefully soon I'll enter the Diaconate life with Jesus taking me there by His hand please pray for me my brothers and sisters for this to happen. Amen.